PROBLEMS OF
PSYCHOANALYTIC TECHNIQUE

PROBLEMS OF
PSYCHOANALYTIC TECHNIQUE

by
OTTO FENICHEL

translated by
DAVID BRUNSWICK

The Psychoanalytic Quarterly, Inc.
57 West 57th Street, New York 19, N. Y.

SIXTH PRINTING

ISBN 0-911194-00-2

Printed in the United States of America

CONTENTS

I. INTRODUCTION 1

II. THE THEORY OF PSYCHOANALYTIC THERAPY 15

III. THE FIRST ANALYTICAL STEPS—DYNAMICS AND ECO-
     NOMICS OF INTERPRETATION 23

IV. STRUCTURAL ASPECTS OF INTERPRETATION 54

V. COMMENTS ON THE ANALYSIS OF THE TRANSFERENCE 71

VI. WORKING THROUGH AND SOME SPECIAL TECHNICAL
     PROBLEMS 76

VII. COMMENTS ON THE LITERATURE OF PSYCHOANALYTIC
     TECHNIQUE 98

     BIBLIOGRAPHY 123

PROBLEMS OF PSYCHOANALYTIC TECHNIQUE

I

Introduction

It might be expected that all the subjects with which psychoanalytic literature deals, questions involving what actually takes place in a psychoanalytic treatment and how the analyst's part therein may be made most effective would predominate. But this expectation does not prove to be correct. Questions of technique are approached in only a small proportion of psychoanalytic writings. This fact may have various causes. In the first place, because the young science of psychoanalysis has as its object of study the totality of human mental phenomena, it must set itself so many questions that the problem of therapeutic technique becomes just one subject among many others. Second, analysts doubtless have a particular aversion to a detailed discussion of this subject, based in part on subjective uncertainty or restraint, but to a greater extent based upon the objective difficulties of the matter itself. A third reason is however the decisive one: the infinite multiplicity of situations arising in analysis does not permit the formulation of general rules about how the analyst should act in every situation, because each situation is essentially unique. Freud[1] therefore declared a long time ago that just as in chess, only the opening moves and some typical concluding situations are teachable, but not all that goes on in between and comprises the actual analytic work.

[1] Freud: *Further Recommendation in the Technique of Psycho-Analysis.* Coll. Papers, Vol. II. London: Hogarth Press, 1933. p. 342.

Nor can this presentation dispel those difficulties inherent in the subject. In the transcript of a course of lectures given in 1936 in Vienna Psychoanalytic Institute, these discussions presuppose in the reader an elementary understanding of analytic technique as well as a knowledge of the general theory of neuroses. They do not attempt to fill the place of a text-book on technique for which the time is not yet ripe, but rather, as the title states, they deal with selected problems of technique.

The selection of problems is such that I am prepared to hear the objection that my discussions are 'too theoretical'. But I know from experience that one circumstance often makes particular difficulties for inexperienced analysts: they may react in their analytic practice in a thoroughly free and elastic manner, and they may also show a good knowledge of the theoretical concepts; however, their practical and their theoretical knowledge remain to a certain extent isolated from each other. It is difficult for them to recognize again the well understood theoretical concepts in what they see and experience in the patient, and still more in what they themselves say and do during the analytic hour.

For this difficulty, I believe, help must and can be given. And this is especially necessary because in psychoanalysis there exists between theory and practice an interesting and particularly important continual reciprocal action. The presence of this reciprocal action is indeed generally recognized but it has not yet been studied in sufficient detail, although as long as sixteen years ago Freud chose exactly this reciprocal action as the subject for a prize competition.[2] With a technical innovation (the abandonment of hypnosis and the introduction of free association) the history of psychoanalytic theory began, and theoretical comprehension of the dynamic-economic interactions of psychic mechanisms made possible the evolution of a technique. Today with the help of psycho-

[2] *Cf.* Int. J. Psa., III, 1922. p. 521.

analytic science, we are in a position not only to understand the origin of neuroses and of character traits, but also to achieve a comprehension of what the analytic therapist does and to judge theoretically the suitability or unsuitability of his actions. It is the task of every theory in all science to lead to better practice. Therefore we will try to use our theory for this purpose and to apply it to our everyday work.

Before organizing our plan for this undertaking, two objecttions must be met which have been repeatedly raised against the formulation of a theory of technique. The one objection is of a very general sort and holds that 'technique' means 'practice', and therefore that a 'theory of technique' would be a 'theory of practice', a contradiction in terms. This is specious logic. Our theory attempts to sum up as general laws of human psychic activity, the facts which have been gathered by the psychoanalytic method in individual instances. What takes place in the analytic procedure can and should be described with the help of these laws just as well as what takes place in any other experience. The second objection, which Reik[3] especially raises, describes more exactly the supposed danger of a 'theory of practice'. Reik believes that such a theoretical description of what goes on in analytic practice is indeed possible, but should play no rôle or only a very small one in training. He believes the grayness of theory might obscure the verdure of the tree of life. If in any of the natural sciences too much theory can mislead the investigator into speculation, this would be the result especially in the still young science of psychology. This has a particular basis in the nature of its subject matter. Scientific comprehension destroys the rich variety of qualitatively colored experience through its tendency toward mere quantitativeness. Psychoanalytic technique can not dispense with intuition which in its empathy with patients requires just the not-reasoned but merely describable abundance of the feelings: psychic reality itself, and not its dead

[3] Reik, Theodor: *New Ways in Psycho-Analytic Technique.* Int. J. Psa., XIV, 1933. pp. 321–334.

conceptual image. It is surprising (from our point of view not at all surprising) that Reik's new book,[4] which emphasizes this attitude so much, gives us the best *theory* of intuition and empathy that we so far have.

When we ask for theory we do not ask for a speculative restriction of the field of vision to a conceptual world instead of reality, just as the physicist does not turn away from reality in his need for theory. We know from the psychology of compulsion neurosis that there can be a flight from the vividness of the world of instinct into the shadow world of words and concepts—a form of defense in which the instincts warded off usually return, changing, for example, an instinctual conflict into a doubting mania. We are familiar also with a flight in the opposite direction: away from unpleasant knowledge into the dark twilight of vague intuition, alien to intellect, with possibilities of magical uses. In a therapeutic method based on science both these types of flight have no place.

Because of the great danger that as a partisan of theory we might be classed with compulsion neurotics, it is worth while to say a little more about the matter. Particularly now that psychoanalytic knowledge is penetrating into broader circles, there often come to us patients who believe they must collect facts from their childhood and interpret dreams. They try to do this in an isolated way with the intellect without any dynamic change in the positions of their instinctual conflicts. We shall speak later about the nature of this resistance and about how to overcome it. There are inexperienced analysts who are subject to the same mistake. When they are promised a 'theory of technique', they expect definite rules of procedure determining all details, prescribing for them the very words that they should speak to the patients. Like compulsion-neurotic patients, these analysts are in danger of substituting theoretical ideas for psychic reality, and probably for the same reason: fear of the real object of their procedure which is the uncovering of instincts and emotions.

[4] Reik, Theodor: *Surprise and the Analyst.* New York: E. P. Dutton & Co., 1937.

But when we emphasize that the analyst must constantly make *use* of his knowledge of the dynamics and economics of psychic life, we want particularly to *prevent* the beginner from allowing his patient to offer him in a state of resistance a discussion of concepts as a substitute for experiences. It is pure supposition that any effort to make analytic technique more systematic means an attempt to replace with sophistry the dynamics of forces; or that the effort to comprehend the task of technique at every point in an analysis from the dynamic-economic point of view is an endeavor to replace 'free floating attention' by continual reflection upon what would then be 'the right thing to do'. There are doubtless some analysts who would like to substitute knowledge for experiences and who therefore do not dissolve repressions but rather play thinking games with their patients. There are perhaps at least as many analysts who commit another equally serious error. They misuse the idea of the analyst's unconscious as the instrument of his perception so that they do hardly any work at all in analysis but just 'float' in it, sit and merely 'experience' things in such a way as to understand fragments of the unconscious processes of the patient and unselectively communicate them to him. Thus there is lacking the oscillation from intuition to understanding and knowledge which alone makes it possible to arrange in a larger context the material which has been understood with the help of the analyst's unconscious. Only in this way can we get a picture of the whole structure of the individual which, even though it is always of a provisional nature and alterable at any time according to new analytic experiences, still determines the order and the nature of our interpretations. The so called 'tact', which determines when and how a given matter is to be revealed to the patient, seems to me *not* the result of a definite biological rhythm as Reik[5] claims, but quite determinable in a systematic way and therefore teachable in a proper degree through comprehension of the definite dynamic changes which take place in the patient during the analysis.

[5] Reik, Theodor: *Ibid.*

It is just this that I wish to try to demonstrate. It is also not correct to state that the rôle of the unconscious as an instrument of knowledge is different in principle in psychoanalysis from what it is in other natural sciences. This difference is reducible to a quantitative one (to be sure a still significant difference) if one is reminded for example of the discovery of the benzene ring in chemistry.[6]

A constant and important task of the analyst is to steer a course between the Scylla of talking instead of experiencing, and the Charybdis of unsystematic 'free floating' that corresponds to the 'acting out' of the patient and is not comprehended by a reasoning power that keeps ulterior aims in view. Therefore we wish to comment in advance somewhat further on this Scylla and Charybdis, before entering into a more detailed discussion of technique.

Let us consider first, the danger of talking instead of experiencing. Words are in general the best means of communicating experiences. But it is well known that they can also be misused for the opposite purpose, that is, to conceal something by 'talking around' it. 'Working in the realm of psychic reality' means preventing such a misuse. We shall have more to say about the fact that this prevention can take place not through shouting and moralizing, but through understanding the origin and tendency of the special type of misuse in the patient in question.

I choose a somewhat extreme example. A patient who has had some previous analysis tells that he is inhibited in automobile driving. Because he has a somewhat indefinite fear of an accident, he turns the steering wheel a little and drives in slightly curved lines instead of straight. He states: 'I know I do that out of sadism, because unconsciously I want to run over everybody'. This interpretation happened not to be correct; the chief cause of his uncertainty was fear of his own excitement in driving, and turning the steering wheel represented an attempt to get out of the car with the car, so to

[6] Robitsek, Alfred: *Symbolisches Denken in der chemischen Forschung.* Imago, I, 1912, pp. 83–90.

speak, by leaving the road. The incorrectness of the interpretation is immaterial; it might have been correct. Such an
interpretation we should certainly not accept gratefully as
insight into his unconscious, but we should ask: 'How do you
know that?' We shall easily be able to show him that his
sadism is not experienced as a reality, but is merely thought
of as a possibility. Thus in the case of the compulsive interpretations of many compulsion neurotics, what will interest us
is not whether the interpretations are correct or not in content, but rather the fact that they are the expression of an
unconscious tendency of the patient to protect himself against
the danger of startling experiences by rapid anticipation of
them in words and thoughts; and we shall attempt to induce
the patient to become aware of his fear of surprises about
which he is as yet ignorant.

In the case of the automobile driver the matter progressed
as follows. At first he held it very much against me that
instead of coöperating with his apparent readiness to analyze,
I exposed it as a resistance, as a symptom of a continual protection against feelings he feared. Then he found the formula:
'But that is exactly my sickness, the fact that I can not admit
such feelings. You should cure me of that. And you demand
as a prerequisite for the cure that I should be able to feel in
the analysis.' Thereupon I tried to make it clear that I did
not make such a 'demand', but that he should search within
himself and see that this not-having-feelings was really a wish-
not-to-have-feelings actively put into play by himself. Such
clarification is most successful when the analyst ferrets out the
weak points in the patient's defense system—those points where
he has in his preconscious, without knowing it and in a displaced and distorted form, the feelings belonging to what he
has said. At these points he can discover the feelings when his
attention is turned in that direction by the analyst's initiative.

It was indeed a great triumph one day in this patient's case
when after the hour had sounded particularly superficial,
insincere, and artificial, he said: 'During the entire hour I
have had a slight feeling of pressure in my abdomen'. The

important thing then was to show him that this feeling of pressure and not the words he had uttered represented the 'associations' we were looking for in that hour—that is, the true derivatives of the unconscious.

'It was not fear', he said, 'only a sort of slight pressure.'

'Like a stomach ache?'

'Not like that either. It was something mental, but not like anxiety. Rather like a nightmare, when one thinks that something is sitting upon one's chest.'

Here we have a good example of defense by means of *negation;* for in a nightmare it is precisely fear that one experiences. Naturally the analysis now progressed to the point of making the patient realize that he was speaking about this feeling of pressure not like a person who is experiencing it, but like a physician who is describing the sensations of a patient in a case history.

This example is a rather gross one but just because of that it shows clearly what we mean by the 'Scylla of talking instead of experiencing'. Study of the theory of technique need not lead to joint speculation with compulsive neurotic patients in lieu of analyzing them. The criteria as to whether or not one is working on the level of 'psychic reality' are indeed nothing else than the 'clicking' that one feels with all 'genuine' utterances of the patient and correct interpretations of the analyst. What 'genuine' means in psychic life would require a separate investigation. For the time being it must suffice to say that it means essentially this: 'passing from impulse to motility without going through a filter of defensive ego'.

A successful piece of analysis, the actual abolition of a defense in the dynamic sense, is characterized as Reik states, by a certain feeling of *surprise* and also by a simplification of the natural arrangement of the material which automatically takes place again and again with each successful gain of new insight. In this way many different matters combine into a unity and things that seemed very separate are shown to belong together and even to be identical with each other. This was not recognized before because they were looked upon previously from different aspects. The 'surprise' does not presuppose, in my opinion, that nothing had been previously thought about the subject in question. The surprise is all the more convincing when it can fill words or thoughts that are already known with a new content of experience. It is always a satisfaction when a patient or a candidate in training analysis who for a long time has known the theory of the œdipus complex or of the castration complex or only the theory of resistance, can say, after an effective hour in which he had not thought about it at all: 'At last I see that these experiences are just what is meant by the œdipus complex (or castration complex or resistance)'.

I shall cite an everyday example of this. When a woman clearly manifests a conflict between a wish to show herself off and an opposing modesty, and when basically it is a fear of disgrace that opposes the exhibitionism, that is, the idea that if she allows herself to be seen her inferiority will become manifest, then we expect according to analytic experience that it is a matter of penis envy, of the fear that her lack of a penis will become evident. But there is a great distance between this concept and the experience of the psychic reality behind it. For example, a woman patient of this type was affected principally by a fear of going insane. It gradually became expressed that by being insane she meant having hallucinations; in other words, she had a compulsive doubt of her own perceptions and was afraid that something she believed she had seen had only been imagined by her. We then learn further that she *wishes* this. She wishes that something that has actually happened *might* only have been imagined. Then the meaning of the fear of insanity changes. To be insane now means to lose control of motility, to notice suddenly that she has already *done* something without having wanted to do it.

We recognize that the motivating fear was something like this:[7]

'Driven by a crazy impulse, I once suddenly did something which I then wished had only been imagined. Therefore I have since been careful and no longer give myself free rein.'

What kind of an act was it? Gradually it becomes clear. She is afraid that if she does not remain continually in control of herself she will throw herself in front of an automobile or out of a window. Therefore the act was something violent. The fear of disgrace further increases to a severe social anxiety. She feels that she is an outcast, that she does not 'belong', that she has poorer clothes than other people. The anxiety becomes noticeably less when she has money in her pocket. She is afraid of being scorned when she has no money and no pretty clothes; and that also means that under those circumstances she is afraid of a sudden violent action of her own.

From this point our knowledge progressed in quite a different, more roundabout way. A disturbance in reading was shown to be caused by compulsive thoughts concerning how the author of the book she was reading might have worked—whether with typewriter, fountain pen, or pencil. She developed an enormous curiosity concerning the methods used by men in productive work, and attempted again and again in vain to identify herself with productive men. It turned out that to watch a productive man meant to do something to him: when she has money, she need not do anything; when she has none, then she wants to take it away from a productive man, that is from one who earns money.

The terrible deed she has committed without wishing to was infantile masturbation which had completely disappeared and was denied because it had been rendered intolerable by the feeling of not being able to perform it the way men do; therefore it had always taken place with fantasies of stealing

[7] I was once reproached with the use of the words, 'something like', in such a context as indicating that I do not take unconscious fantasies seriously. I deny this. Its use means that the unconscious fantasies are *vague*, and therefore can only be reproduced in words inexactly, always with the addition of 'something like'.

a penis. Now for the first time the patient recognized with 'surprise' that penis envy, about which she had always known theoretically, was a *psychic reality*.

Now to a consideration of the Charybdis. Psychic reality must be carefully worked through. Fear of the Scylla of theoretical discussion has led to an overvaulation of emotional eruptions, to a failure to recognize that such 'abreactions' can also serve the resistance. They allow derivatives of the unconscious to go up in smoke while not the slightest change is effected in the real pathogenic conflict. Not only do 'spurious emotional eruptions' exist (just as there is a 'spurious lack of affect'), but even 'genuine' ones are of themselves no guarantee for definitely breaking through the defenses.

We must remember what power is wielded in human thinking by *magic,* a technique which welcomes great dramatic events as magical ceremonies and proofs of magical effectiveness; and we must remember why such magic is a constant enemy of analysis. 'Surprise effects the cure.' This formula is misused by many patients' expectations of magic derived from the resistance. And something dangerous in the psyche of the analyst coöperates with this expectation of magic: the temptation to play prophet always looms large.

We are reminded of Bleuler's[8] concept of 'autistic thinking', which plays such a large rôle in medicine. One need only to take up at random any clinical journal and compare it with any journal of chemistry or physics; then one must in the name of medicine feel ashamed before every chemist and physicist. This is due to the traditions of medicine which descend directly from the medicine men, the priests. Psychiatry or psychopathology is in turn the youngest of the subjects in the realm of medicine to be wrested from magic. It was not very long ago that anatomists were not allowed to dissect the human body. The opposition to such activities comes from the rebellion of human beings against having to become only a part of nature.

[8] Bleuler, Eugen: *Das autistisch-undisziplinierte Denken in der Medizin und seine Überwindung.* Berlin: Julius Springer, 1927.

To be sure, after man became free in the physical sphere, it was not psychoanalysis that made the first attempt to rescue the psychic sphere from the grasp of magic and make it accessible to scientific investigation. But the attempts that were made before the advent of psychoanalysis were either pseudo-materialism of the sort which could say: 'The psyche is only a secretion of the brain'; [9] or else the attempts were those of an 'experimental psychology' which restricted itself to the study of isolated functions in a manner remote from life. A scientific comprehension of the true complications of every-day human psychic life really began only with psychoanalysis. Frequently the reverse is stated: in contrast to the rationalism of a Virchow, it is said, Freud was the first to gain recognition for the irrational, the psychogenic. And that is true; but in what way is it true? Did he conquer a new realm for natural science, or did he reject an unjustified presumption of natural science? Both are true. The Virchow era was perhaps not so scientific as it thought. Shutting its eyes to the existence of the psyche cannot be interpreted as a sign of its scientism. The psyche was at that time still a domain reserved for re-ligion and magic; no scientist bothered himself about it. Omitting the psyche was the compromise that enabled the investigators to be scientists. They were conscious scientists but unconscious mystics in psychology. Freud turned atten-tion again to the psyche, and thereby won it more honestly for science than did the 'secretion materialists'. If this is true of psychology in general, the remnants of magic are still much stronger in psychotherapy, and the temptation to be a magician is no less than the temptation to have oneself cured by a magician.

Psychoanalytic technique is a complicated task. Its tool is the unconscious of the analyst which intuitively compre-hends the unconscious of the patient. Its aim is to lift this comprehension out of intuition into scientific clarity. Analytic

[9] This is as if, after the discovery that the bile is a secretion of the liver, only the histology of the liver and not the physiological chemistry of the bile were considered to be science.

therapy requires from the physician 'on the one hand . . . the free play of association and fantasy, the full indulgence of *his own unconscious;* on the other hand the physician must subject the material submitted by himself and the patient to a logical scrutiny and in his dealings and communications must let himself be guided *exclusively* by the results of this mental effort'.[10] This logical activity is disregarded when 'the lack of all system', 'the absence of any definite plan' is recommended, and reason called 'a completely unsuitable instrument for the investigation of the unconscious mental processes'. Such formulations run counter to the purpose of psychoanalysis, which is to win such investigation for the cause of reason. The subject matter, not the method, of psychoanalysis is irrational.

Comparison with surgical technique is quite to the point. One who has a thorough command of topographical anatomy but no surgical technique cannot operate. Nor can one successfully operate who is a born surgeon but knows nothing about topographical anatomy. Talent is not teachable, whereas topographical anatomy is. In a course in psychoanalytic technique the topographical anatomy of the psyche can and should be taught.

We have a dynamic and economic conception of psychic life. Therefore our technique which strives for a dynamic and economic change in the patient, must also follow dynamic and economic principles. It must adhere consistently to the mode of thinking underlying all psychoanalysis, and the procedure arising from intuition, which to be sure is indispensable, must be arranged according to rational criteria.

We see from the few discussions about technique in the literature that opinion is extremely divergent, and that even opinions about the therapeutically effective factors differ very widely, as the symposium[11] at the Marienbad Congress revealed. This, it seems to me, is not only a consequence of

---

[10] Ferenczi, Sandor: On the Technique of Psycho-Analysis. In *Further Contributions to the Theory and Technique of Psycho-Analysis*. London: Hogarth Press, 1926. p. 189.

[11] *Symposium on the Theory of the Therapeutic Results of Psycho-Analysis.* Int. J. Psa., XVIII, 1937. pp. 125–189.

the fact that the personalities of various analysts express themselves differently in practice, but also of the fact that there are often uncertainties as to the governing principles which should be common to all analysts despite differences in personality—if the various methods are still to be called analytic. This state of affairs exists because the task of clarifying a theory of technique according to rational criteria has been insufficiently developed.   Hence we shall try in this paper to further this development, and to do so with constant reference to practice, and subject to constant correction through practical experience.

Systematic procedure requires insight into the aims to be attained and into the ways leading thereto.   Even though historically analytic practice did not originate deductively from the theory of analytic therapy, the latter has today progressed so far that its practice can be made clear to the student in this deductive way.   Alexander [12] rightly says that most of the proposals for the reform of technique come from authors who wish to elevate as the sole means of salvation some one of the many mechanisms involved in the process of analytic therapy. It should ultimately be possible to determine what is essential and what is merely accidental; therefore I believe that we must begin with a survey of the nature of analytic therapy; then we can examine the ways of arriving at the unconscious and making it accessible, especially the dynamics and economics of interpretation.   Our findings on those points will then be a basis for our investigation of the handling of the transference, in which questions concerning so called ego analysis and id analysis will become clear to us. We shall then discuss 'working through', specific questions such as the 'activity' of the analyst, the connection between present reality and childhood, prognostic criteria, and other similar problems. Finally we shall present a critical survey of the literature on the subject of psychoanalytic technique.

[12] Alexander, Franz: *The Problem of Psychoanalytic Technique.* The Psa. Quarterly, IV, 1935. pp. 588–611.

II

The Theory of Psychoanalytic Therapy

Neurosis is a complicated phenomenon. One can get one's bearings in a complicated subject only if one adopts, as a basis, a definite system of orientation with definite coördinates to which to refer all phenomena.

Psychoanalysis approaches the neurosis as it does all psychic phenomena, with the fundamental assumption that the original function of the psychic apparatus is to discharge entering quantities of excitation and later on, to bind them. If this fails, undischargeable quantities will flood the apparatus in an unbound form. That is the prerequisite for a neurosis: an escape-discharge not willed by the ego, taking place through unusual channels. We shall disregard the purely traumatic neuroses in which the excitation has flooded the apparatus by virtue of too big a supply per unit of time. In the psycho-neuroses the damming up has come about through insufficient discharge because of a chronic defense of the ego against the instincts. Since we can therapeutically influence only the ego, there are in principle only two possibilities for such influence: we can try to strengthen the ego in such a way that it more successfully carries out its defense against instinct, or we can bring the ego to give up the defense or to replace it by a more suitable one. Actually there exist combinations of these two logically contradictory methods. We can, for example, strengthen the defense against a certain instinctual impulse by providing a derivative of it with a discharge. By this partial discharge the instinct becomes relatively weaker, and the work of defense against the remainder becomes easier. Since the symptom itself also represents such a displacement substitute, which somewhat relieves the pressure of the pathogenic instinct (primary gain from illness), we may say that the above-mentioned combinations of therapeutic method artificially imitate the genesis of neurosis and replace the neurosis which is to be combated by an artificial one. Such an artificial neurosis is presumably both the 'rapport' in hypnosis and the transference in the course of psychoanalysis. Glover [13] designated as 'artificial compulsion neuroses' the therapies of neurosis based on definite tasks which the patient must perform, such as following rules of diet or behavior; he designated as 'artificial phobias' the methods giving the patient psychic part-truths which he accepts as a substitute for the whole truth, just as the phobic person accepts the idea of the street as a substitute for the idea of temptation; and as 'artificial paranoias' the treatments of neurosis by medicines, provided that the medicine is regarded as a 'good introjected object'.

Direct suggestion strengthens the repression; indirect suggestion is, as has been shown, something intermediate between strengthening and eliminating repression. Analysis operates *in principle* in the second manner, namely, by doing away with the defense or replacing it with a really suitable one. Therefore we have two questions to answer: first, by what means is the ego actuated to give up or modify the defense against instinct; second, how shall we explain in dynamic and economic terms the changes occurring after the abandonment or modification of the defense against instinct?

The motive for a pathogenic defense against instinct is always in the last analysis an estimate of the danger of an aroused instinct, the fear of the displeasure that would ensue if one were to yield to his instincts. The belief in such a danger has a variety of origins. Essentially it corresponds to the child's *experiences,* though to be sure in part to experiences which have been misinterpreted. It is the reality principle which teaches the child that the pleasure of instinctual gratification must under certain circumstances be paid for by displeasure of another sort. It is discipline, forbidding instinctual satisfaction which then artificially amplifies this reality principle to an extreme degree, and it is the projective misunderstanding of the objective and the educating environment

[13] Glover, Edward: *The Therapeutic Effect of Inexact Interpretation.* Int. J. Psa., XII, 1931. pp. 397–411.

which creates the frightfulness of the punishments that are unconsciously expected to follow transgression of the prohibitions.

Whether the danger actually threatens from the external world or is already introjected is inessential. Therefore Freud in The Problem of Anxiety [14] designated as the essence of the neurosis, the retention of anxieties beyond the period when they are physiologically normal. The retention of a belief in a danger not objectively present is however itself a consequence of the defense against instinct effected in childhood under the influence of that very anxiety. Along with the portions of instincts warded off, the anxiety too, which led to the defense, has become unconscious and has lost its connection with the total personality. It does not participate in the development of the rest of the ego and is not corrected by later experiences.

We must not forget that in later life there are various deprivations from without which are suited to remobilize the old anxieties. This can come about either directly, in case the depriving circumstances are looked upon as confirmations of the old anxieties; or indirectly, in case the deprivation causes a regression and the resulting change of adult into infantile sexuality remobilizes the anxieties that were opposed to the infantile sexuality. But not all the precipitating causes of neurotic illness in later life are real deprivations. They can also be, for example, special opportunities for satisfactions or anything at all that is calculated either to increase the relative proportion of infantile sexuality within the total sexuality, or cause the anxiety opposed to the sexuality to appear more justified. The fantastic character of this anxiety is then due to the circumstance that, continuing to exist unaltered outside of the domain of the ego, it is exempt from correction by experience.

The therapeutic task then is to reunite with the conscious

14 Freud, Sigmund: *The Problem of Anxiety.* New York: The Psa. Quarterly Press and W. W. Norton & Co., 1936. p. 119.

ego the contents (both portions of instinct and unconscious anxieties of the ego) which have been withheld from consciousness and the total personality by countercathexes of the ego, and to abolish the effectiveness of the countercathexes.[15] This is made possible through the circumstance that the instinct components warded off produce *derivatives*. If we follow the fundamental rule of psychoanalysis and thus exclude as far as possible the purposive tendencies of the ego, these derivatives which are always to be observed in the impulses of human beings become still clearer. Every interpretation, either of a resistance or of an id impulse, consists in demonstrating a derivative as such to the judging portion of the ego against the resistance. It is not interpretation simply to name unconscious contents not yet represented by a preconscious derivative which can be recognized as such by the patient merely by turning his attention to it. All this we shall elucidate in detail in what follows. Likewise we shall discuss in detail how the demonstration to the patient that he is defending himself, how he defends himself, why he does it, and what the defense is directed against, must act as an education of the defending ego to a tolerance of more and more undistorted derivatives. In discussing what in practice is the most important instance of interpretation—the interpretation of the transference resistance—Sterba [16] has shown how it becomes effective through a sort of splitting of the ego into a reasonable judging portion and an experiencing portion, the former recognizing the latter as not appropriate in the present and as coming from the past. This leads to a reduction in anxiety and consequently to a production of further, more undistorted

[15] This seems a matter of course, but we shall see that it is by no means clear to everybody; otherwise it would also be clear that all coercive methods in which such union does not succeed, and all attempts not to confront an ego with unconscious contents through interpretations but to establish a reasonable ego through interpretations when it is lacking, are in principle not analytic.

[16] Sterba, Richard: *Zur Dynamik der Bewältigung des Übertragungswiderstandes.* Int. Ztschr. Psa., XV, 1929. [Eng. trans. The Psa. Quarterly, IX, No. 3, 1940. Ed.]

derivatives.[17] The cleavage is accomplished by utilizing the positive transference and transitory identifications with the analyst.

Certain fundamental technical rules such as, 'analysis starts always from the surface of the present', 'interpretation of resistance precedes interpretation of content', and the like, follow from what has been said as a matter of course. I postpone at this point such important questions as 'interpretation of resistance versus interpretation of content', 'ego analysis versus id analysis', confining myself now to principles. In principle there is no difference between these two types of interpretation; unconscious resistances cannot be eliminated otherwise than by demonstration of their conscious derivatives and the forms in which they appear—just as with id-contents; and the timely naming of warded off id impulses which have already become noticeable to the more tolerant ego, works also by eliminating defense activities of the ego.

The 'analytic atmosphere', which convinces the patient that he has nothing to fear in tolerating impulses formerly warded off, seems not only to be a prerequisite for any transference interpretation (for if the analyst shared in any way in the patient's reactions, the fact that the patient's feelings are determined by his past could not be demonstrated) but it is also an important means of persuading the ego to accept on trial something formerly repelled.

The fear expressed by Kaiser [18] that this might lead to an isolation of the analysis from real life, the patient feeling that here he is only playing at his impulses, whereas in real life where they are in earnest, he must continue to defend himself against them, seems to me occasionally well founded; in such cases we must analyze this resistance. But this objection is not

---

[17] It remains to be investigated how this desirable 'splitting of the ego' and 'self-observation' are to be differentiated from the pathological cleavage and self-observation which is directed at preserving isolations and serves to *prevent* the production of derivatives.

[18] Kaiser, Hellmuth: *Probleme der Technik*. Int. Ztschr. Psa., XX, 1934. pp. 490–522.

sufficient to counteract the advantages of the atmosphere of tolerance. 'Acting out', which impedes the ego from being confronted with unconscious material, often affords the analyst valuable insight. However, it seems in principle to be no less a danger than the contrasting sort of 'theoretical analysis' which talks about the past without noting that it is still present, because 'acting out' relates only to the present and does not make the patient conscious of being dominated by his past. Analysis should show the past to be effective in the present. Freud once said that when the patient talks only of his present reality, the analyst must speak of his childhood; and the analyst must bring in present reality when the patient relates only childhood reminiscences. Theorizing about childhood relates only to a past that is not connected up with present reality, whereas 'acting out' is present reality, the past character of which is not evident.

Freud [19] said that in analysis we induce the ego by all methods of suggestion to let up in the production of defenses. In practice this is certainly still true today, and the utilization of the transference for this purpose is after all nothing but suggestion. Still we must say that we obtain the desired effect upon the patient all the more lastingly and efficaciously if we succeed in using no other means of eliminating resistances than the confrontation of his reasonable ego with the fact of his resistance and the history of its origin. This confrontation bringing him as it does recognition of the unconscious part of his resistance, also renders the resistance itself superfluous.

Certainly there occurs in practice a gradual entrance of the analyst into the superego of the patient, such as takes place in hypnosis, and such as Strachey [20] considers characteristic also for analytic therapy. There occur, too, all those 'effects of inexact interpretation' investigated by Glover,[21] i.e., the pos-

19 Freud: *A General Introduction To Psychoanalysis*. New York: Liveright Publ. Co., 1935. p. 392 ff.

20 Strachey, James: *The Nature of the Therapeutic Action of Psycho-Analysis*. Int. J. Psa., XV, 1934. pp. 127–160.

21 Glover, Edward: *The Therapeutic Effect of Inexact Interpretation*. Loc. cit.

sibility of bringing about substitute discharges for the diminishing neurotic discharges either in transference actions or in other phenomena afforded by the cure.

If we succeed in this way in abolishing the pathogenic defense activity of the ego, what is the result? Since neurotics are persons who in their unconscious instinctual life have either remained on an infantile level or have regressed to it, that is, persons whose sexuality (or aggression) has retained infantile forms, we might theoretically expect perversions as the result of such therapy. Anna Freud [22] believes indeed that in children psychoanalytic influence must really be combined with a pedagogical one, because otherwise the removal of a repression directed against anal erotism, for example, would lead to smearing with fæces. She believes also [23] that in the case of many adults who have set up their defenses because of fear of the excessive quantity of their instinctual energy, the elimination of the defense might lead to the eruption of this excessive quantity and to the overwhelming of the entire ego. Practice, I believe, teaches us that there is no such danger. The warded off portions of instincts have retained their infantile character only because they were warded off and have thereby lost their connection with the total personality. In the meantime the personality has developed further. If the energy which was bound up in the defense struggle is joined again to the personality, it fits itself in with it and with the genital primacy arrived at by it. The pregenital sexuality, freed from entanglement in the defense struggle, is thereby changed into genital sexuality capable of orgasm. It is primarily the experiences of satisfaction now made possible, that once and for all abolish the pathogenic damming-up.[24] Single 'abreactions' cannot accomplish this. They give momentary

[22] Freud, Anna: *The Technique of Child Analysis.* New York & Washington: Nerv. & Ment. Dis. Publ. Co., 1928. pp. 42–59.

[23] Freud, Anna: *The Ego and the Mechanisms of Defense.* London: Hogarth Press, 1938.

[24] Instinctual excitations are *periodic* processes, which after satisfaction disappear for a time and only gradually accumulate again. If the individual's apparatus for satisfaction functions adequately, the ego need have no particular 'fear of an excessive quantity of instinct'.

relief but no abolition of the defense struggle and no liberation of the energy bound up in it. This relative belittling of the therapeutic importance of 'abreactions' and of the 'dissipation of repressed instinctual excitations in the act of becoming conscious'—in contrast to facilitating the development of a well regulated sexual economy—is also what causes us to value relatively little the therapeutic effect of the single eruption of affect, however much it is to be welcomed in some analytic situations. On the other hand we value very highly the therapeutic importance of the subsequent 'working through'. This 'working through', according to Rado comparable to the work of mourning, consists in demonstrating again and again the unconscious impulse, once it has been recognized, in its manifold forms and connections, and in attaining thereby the effective cessation of the pathogenic instinct defense. It is true that other kinds of discharge which were heretofore impossible, namely sublimations, become possible through the abolition of the defense. Quantitatively they play a lesser rôle for the adjustment of the instinctual processes of the formerly neurotic personality than does adequate sexual satisfaction.[25]

25 The questions of 'working through' and the possibility of sublimation will be discussed in more detail later on.

III

The First Analytical Steps—Dynamics and Economics of Interpretation

Up to this point we have determined how psychoanalysis operates *in principle:* it demonstrates derivatives of the unconscious as such, and thereby induces a tolerance of the derivatives which become less and less distorted. Gradually it confronts the ego with contents previously warded off and abolishes the division between these isolated contents and the personality as a whole. It allows the instincts warded off to catch up with the development which the ego has passed through in the meantime, changing infantile into adult sexuality, and thus makes possible a well regulated sexual economy. It leads to 'condemnations' of certain instinctual satisfactions by the reasonable ego and, finally, to sublimations. Everything else is incidental.

What are the practical details of this process? What happens after a patient lies on the couch? Here I make a digression to ask another question: should the patient lie down at all? The advantages of the usual position of the patient, recommended by Freud,[26] are clear; it allows the patient relative relaxation, and makes it easier for him to say unpleasant things because he does not face the analyst; and the analyst himself is saved the discomfort of having to control his own facial expressions. To these advantages is opposed a disadvantage: the observance of a prescribed 'ceremonial' produces a 'magical' impression and may be misinterpreted by the patient in this sense. We know, however, that in general the advantages preponderate but that we can and must be *elastic* in the application of all technical rules.

[26] Freud: *Further Recommendations in the Technique of Psychoanalysis.* Coll. Papers, II. London: Hogarth Press, 1933. p. 354.

Everything is permissible, if only one knows why. Not external measures, but the management of resistance and transference is the criterion for estimating whether a procedure is analysis or not. There may be one of two reasons for deviating from the usual position. First, the patient may not want to lie down. As a rule, we do not yield to resistances but analyze them. However, there are exceptions to this rule: if a patient has an agoraphobia, we will not require him before the beginning of the analysis to ignore his fear and go out into the street. We must estimate to what degree the patient can endure opposing his phobic restrictions. If we have the impression that a patient *cannot* lie down and would rather forego the analysis than do so, we will allow him to sit. We must then take care that he is not permitted to observe the phobic avoidance strictly as a new sense of security; we must insist that this subject be talked about. Second, the patient may be too eager to lie down. The magical character of lying down can be utilized for resistance in such a way that analysis and life become isolated from one another and the patient vaguely feels that what he says while lying down is no longer valid when he stands up. Some patients, otherwise timid, are impudent on the couch. So an analysis may apparently run smoothly, but actually only on the condition that the patient is lying down. The exclusive use of this position may nullify the effectiveness it usually has. Just as some patients go to the toilet before or after the analytic hour or perform some other specific act which separates the hour from the rest of their lives, so the external situation of analysis serves the same purpose for others. The analyst must *interpret* the resistance with reference to this purpose. In many cases we support the interpretation by having the patient sit down and so demonstrate to him how differently he feels in the new situation. Often the information that analysis can also be conducted with the patient in a sitting position suffices to make the patient realize that to him 'analysis' and 'reality' are different and an actual change of position is not necessary. Freud [27] has pointed out how important it is to frustrate the attempt by some patients to divide the visit to the analyst into 'official' and 'unofficial' parts by saying a few more words to the analyst after the termination of the hour. This attempt should be frustrated, according to Freud, by drawing the 'unofficial' remarks into the next 'official' hour. But just as often the opposite measure is useful in eliminating the resistance of isolation. The continuation, even for a moment, of an interpretation or a conversation begun in the hour, when the patient is no longer lying down, is often a very effective demonstration that analysis concerns the individual's entire life even when he does not happen to be lying on a couch.

We now return to our question: what happens after a patient lies down? He begins to talk. As we know, he can say whatever he wants. If he has symptoms, he will in most cases begin with them, otherwise with present difficulties that trouble him. If he has neither of these, he will begin with trifles of the moment that occupied him just as the hour began. Symptoms and present difficulties predominate among the subjects chosen because the patient is aware that he consults the analyst for a definite *purpose*. If he does too much talking about his symptoms and never gets away from the conscious description of his difficulties, then we recognize that as a resistance which requires special handling. But even aside from this resistance, the fact remains that the 'free associations' of analysands always retain an aspect determined by the conscious awareness of the purpose of the whole analysis. This knowledge, the wish for recovery, is of the greatest importance as a motive for overcoming the resistances. Its significance may be observed in cases where it is lacking. In such cases it is necessary, before the analysis, to alienate from the rest of the patient's ego the pathological conduct which is not yet felt to be pathological. If a reasonable ego from which such con-

[27] *Ibid.*, pp. 359-360.

duct could be alienated is also lacking, then analysis is in principle impossible, and a preanalytic pedagogical training is required to establish such a reasonable ego. In practice, however, such an ego is never completely lacking, and initial analytic steps to extend gradually the ego domain are made possible by utilizing the residual ego. This seems to me the only possibility. I do not understand just what can be meant by a 'surprise attack on the patient in which one gets into direct contact with his id'.

There is undoubtedly also a *pathological* wish for recovery. Nunberg [28] has devoted a paper to it. It consists of the patient's magical hopes: *(a)* he strives for a strengthening of his neurotic equilibrium; *(b)* he hopes to get infantile wish fulfilments from the analysis.

With reference to the former, it may be stated that many people develop towards others no real object relationships, but use other people to solve or alleviate their intrapsychic conflicts. For example: the defiant man leads another person to do him an injustice so that he can make use of the injustice as a weapon against his superego; other people, for the same reason, strive for proofs of being loved, in order to cite the forgiveness therein implied in an 'appeal' from condemnation by their superego; the liar calls the hearer of his lies to witness in an intrapsychic conflict between remembering and a tendency to repress. Sometimes love is used to satisfy the most varied narcissistic needs and to relieve intrapsychic tensions.[29] For such purposes the analyst too can be used by the patient. He does not want from the analysis a liberation from the crutches of his former neurotic equilibrium. He expects stronger crutches.

[28] Nunberg, Herman: *Über den Genesungswunsch.* Int. Ztschr. f. Psa., XI, 1925. pp. 179–193.

[29] Incidentally, insofar as such narcissistic requirements play a part in love, the latter is *disordered;* when Jekels and Bergler (*Übertragung und Liebe.* Imago, XX, 1934. pp. 5–31) describe precisely these narcissistic needs as the essence of love reactions, they are dealing with the *pathology* and not the psychology of love.

The patient's hope to get from the analysis infantile wish fulfilment is exemplified by the expectation that in 'getting well' an early need for revenge will at last find satisfaction. Here belong the 'exceptions' described by Freud,[30] who expect that the special consideration from fate which they believe they deserve, will begin with their 'getting well'. In particular, one finds women who expect that after the analysis they will at last possess a penis.

Such pathological wishes for recovery can be favorable to the analysis as motives for overcoming resistances, *but only to a certain degree*. At some point the *irrational* element they contain will become a resistance. Reik [31] once expressed the opinion that the utterance of tabooed words can alone have a curative effect through belief in the omnipotence of words. But the analyst is *not* omnipotent. If he relies on a belief in omnipotence as a curative factor, he has fallen into the Charybdis of 'floating' in emotional experiences without the aid of his reasoning power, and this must ultimately have its unfortunate consequences.

What is true of the pathological wish for recovery is equally true of the so called positive transference. Incidentally, one must doubt whether a division of transference forms into 'positive' and 'negative' is accurate. The transference forms occurring in neurotics are distinguished by their ambivalence; that is, they are as a rule at the same time positive and negative, or at least they can easily turn from one form into the other. In so far as they express resistance in analysis, we may call both of them 'irrational transference'. If, on the other hand, we should wish to designate as 'rational' transference the 'aim-inhibited positive transference' suitable for analysis, such an expression would seem to be self-contradictory; for transference is bound up with the fact that a person does not react

30 Freud: *Some Character Types Met With in Psycho-Analytic Work*. Coll. Papers, IV. London: Hogarth Press, 1934. pp. 319–323.

31 Reik, Theodor: *Surprise and the Analyst*. New York: E. P. Dutton & Co., 1937.

rationally to the influences of the outer world but reads past situations into them. So the positive transference, like the pathological wish for recovery, may be very welcome during long periods of an analysis as a motive for overcoming resistances; but *in so far as it is transference,* the impulses belong to infantile objects, and therefore a time must come when these same transference impulses become resistances, and their true relationship must be demonstrated to the patient.

Pathological conceptions of getting well may in some cases function as resistance from the beginning of an analysis. This is the case when a defense which is directed against a forbidden impulse is also directed against the conception of recovery, because recovery means gratification of the forbidden impulse. Many 'negative therapeutic reactions' result from the fact that the patient prefers his *status quo,* full of displeasure as it is, as the lesser evil, as better than a change to health which is perceived as a feared instinct satisfaction.

To return to our main theme, the wish for recovery and the knowledge of the real purpose of the analysis always impart to the free associations of the patient the most *general* sort of purposeful tendency. Apart from that, we seek by means of the fundamental rule to eliminate purposeful tendencies as much as possible. However, I should like to interpolate here the opinion that it is questionable whether it is good to charge all prospective patients with the observance of the fundamental rule as early as the preliminary consultation or the beginning of the first analytic session. While we still do not know the patient, it is possible that we are imposing such a task upon a person with a brooding mania, in which case we make our work very difficult. Therefore I usually say at first merely that the patient must tell me a great deal about himself before I can tell him anything, and it would not be sensible if he did not try to be entirely honest in his communications. An opportunity can then soon be found to make the rest clear in a manner suited to the individual case.

I should like to yield to the temptation to digress again,

and before the discussion of the theory of free association, to consider other questions concerning the preliminary consultation. The rule that the patient should not make vital decisions during the analysis, I usually present only after I know the patient better and can be sure that he does not unconsciously hear such an admonition as a parental prohibition or even as a castration threat. To be sure, it is good practice to present this rule as soon as possible in the case of persons with a tendency to 'acting out', since it would be too late after a certain vital question has already become the representative of a definite unconscious conflict.

Another question is how to construe the rule that 'analytic treatment should be carried through, as far as is possible, in a state of abstinence'. I believe that in respect to this rule no misunderstanding is possible.[32] A *symptom* is a *substitute* for something repressed, and when in place of it another substitute a little more pleasant beckons to the patient, he gladly accepts it and is content with it. We are reminded of the account by Glover,[33] already cited, concerning 'artificial compulsion neuroses, hysterias, and paranoias'. This holds true particularly for the transference. If the analysis becomes a *game* of any sort, if the daily hour is in itself some satisfaction for the patient, then he will only hold on to this bit of satisfaction and nothing drives him further. Therefore the analyst must not offer his patients any *transference satisfactions*. ('Playing along' with the transference actions of the patients is contraindicated for other reasons too, to be discussed later.) The fulfilment of what the patient longs for most in the analysis serves as a resistance to further analysis and therefore must be refused him.

In the case of patients who 'act out', it sometimes occurs that such insufficient 'provisional satisfactions' burst forth out-

[32] Freud: *Turnings in the Ways of Psycho-Analytic Therapy*. Coll. Papers, II. London: Hogarth Press, 1933. pp. 396 ff.

[33] Glover, Edward: *The Therapeutic Effect of Inexact Interpretation*. Int. J. Psa., XII, 1931. pp. 397–411.

side the frame of the analysis. If we can demonstrate to the patient the resistance character of such actions, all is well; if not, we will under certain circumstances invoke the 'rule of abstinence' in this situation, too, and advise him to abstain from the actions in question.   In the same way we must induce the phobic patient at a certain point in the analysis to subject himself to the displeasure of the phobic situation. In this respect perverts and addicts present a special problem, because their symptoms are pleasureful in themselves and are already a portion of 'substitute satisfaction'; and when certain 'secondary gains' are present, we find the same situation in the case of ordinary neurotic symptoms.   We can in these cases advise the patient to abstain from those activities that are detrimental to the analysis but we should know that this advice cannot be of much benefit at first, because the patient for the time being knows no other forms of pleasure.   If he could give up his symptoms upon a mere command, he would not need analysis.

However, we also hear another interpretation of the 'rule of abstinence' than the one I have presented.   There are analysts who want completely to forbid their patients any sexual activity, or at least sexual activity under certain circumstances, such as extramarital or premarital intercourse.   What do they really expect from such an attitude?   Do they believe they can silence a physiological function with a prohibition? And do they consider it desirable to eliminate and to surround with a prohibiting atmosphere the very function which analysis seeks to restore, to free from prohibitions and supervise in its advancing liberation?   Do they believe that they are furthering the analysis when they renew the sexual prohibitions of parents and other educators which have driven the patient into his neurosis?   We hear of such prohibiting advice especially against masturbation.   But unfortunately the analyst cannot do away with an obstacle to his work so conveniently.   If masturbation disturbs the analysis, we have to analyze the connection between masturbation and analysis.

We return to our earlier question: what do we expect from the fundamental rule? In human beings there are always many unconscious impulses which wish to express themselves, pushing constantly towards consciousness and towards motility, and others, the defensive tendencies of the ego, acting in the opposite direction. In this play of forces present stimuli continually interfere. None of these stimuli remains quite without connection with the unconscious impulses that are constantly in search of 'representatives'. The response to an indifferent outer stimulus can therefore, according to the circumstances, become either a *derivative* of an unconscious impulse, or in case it is recognized in that rôle, once more the object of a defense.[34] These connections between present reality and unconscious impulses are particularly strong in the neurotic. The neurotic is characterized precisely by never reacting to outer stimuli appropriately, but always according to definite patterns or reaction acquired in the course of his childhood. If the actions, impulses, and associations of human beings are fed always both by present realities and the past, in the case of the neurotic the past always predominates because, not differentiating sufficiently between the two, he always misunderstands the present in the sense of his unsolved past, and that includes both his present instinctual impulses as well as present external reality.

Into the conglomeration of past and present, of derivatives that want to express themselves, and of the reality principle that determines what is now allowed to be expressed, the *ego* as representative of reality is constantly stepping in with definite ideas of *purpose*. What one wants to say or do right now, suppresses all impulses that do not belong to this purpose. (The absence of this suppression, determined by the purpose of the moment, is a specific problem in the psychology of mania.) The ego is continually selecting, in a modifying way,

[34] Freud: *The Unconscious.* Coll. Papers, IV. London: Hogarth Press, 1934. pp. 122 ff.

from numerous impulses constantly emerging. Fuchs [35] rightly
points out that we should speak not of a 'dream work', but
rather of a 'work of the waking state'; for the psychic events
that take place in accordance with the primary process run
their course relatively automatically, but the ego constantly
intervenes with a special expenditure of energy in order to
subject these psychic events to the secondary process.

By observance of the fundamental rule we attempt to eliminate as much as possible the regulating activity of the ego
described above. Then the 'derivatives' of the unconscious
must become more clearly recognizable as such. At the same
time we endeavor to exclude special outer stimuli which could
influence the patient's impulses in a particular direction or
effect an undesired selection among them. When the analyst,
by means of irritating remarks, *provokes* a display of emotion
in the patient, we may not speak of this emotional display
as 'transference'; at least we shall not be able to demonstrate
as such the portion of transference which must of course be
present in such an affect too. When, for example, we are
striving to demonstrate to the patient in their true function,
certain character traits of his which serve as resistance, and
for this purpose we imitate him, we are likely thereby to injure
his narcissism. If then he becomes angry, we have not thus
'liberated his negative transference', but have simply made
him angry.

What do we see then when a patient sincerely strives to
exclude his 'purposive tendencies' by following the fundamental rule of free association? We can thus eliminate, to
be sure, very many interferences of the ego, but not the
strongest ones. The 'resistances' remain. Precisely those
defenses against instinct which were pathogenetic are inacces-
sible to the conscious will, and often enough the patient is
not aware that they are effective. What we then catch sight
of is the expression of a conflict, the alternate approaching

35 Fuchs, S. H. *Zum Stand der heutigen Biologie*. Imago, XXII, 1936.
pp. 210–241.

and receding of the unconscious impulse. The patient knows nothing of the fact that what he is saying is the expression of such a conflict.

Thus we see that the 'resistance' remains effective even when the fundamental rule is applied. What is resistance? We could say it is the force that has caused the pathogenic defense. But does not this answer oversimplify the matter? Freud [36] indeed has said that there are five kinds of resistance. But the division into these five kinds of resistance was, as Freud himself emphasized, quite unsystematic. In principle we can, I believe, adhere to the equating of 'resistance' with 'resistance of defense' or, as Freud says, 'resistance of repression'.

Let us with this in mind examine the four other kinds of resistance:

(1) The *resistances due to secondary gains* are, it is true, something else. They are often extensive and decisive for the technique of many analyses; but after all they are also a concern of the ego and are more likely to be accessible to the conscious will.

(2) *Transference resistance* is not to be contrasted with 'resistance of repression'. It is true that transference actions frequently look like impulses of the id, but the fact that such impulses are resistance is due to the destruction of the context to which they belong, to the incorrect place at which they appear, and to the compromise character which they receive through the intervention of the defending ego.

(3) The *superego resistance,* I believe, in the same way does not proceed from the superego, but from the ego, which tries to yield to a prompting of the superego. There are manifold conflicts between ego and superego. We cannot at all explain, for instance, the phenomena of compulsion neurosis without assuming a 'double countercathexis'—one against the id and one against the superego. The resistance activities proceeding from the superego are fundamentally only a variety of resistance of repression.

36 Freud: *The Problem of Anxiety.* New York: The Psa. Quarterly Press and W. W. Norton & Co., 1936. pp. 138–139.

(4) There remains the so called *resistance of the id,* of which we shall speak separately.

We see then in free associations a to-and-fro struggle between instinct derivatives and defenses, wherein the topics of the symptoms present difficulties and everyday trifles predominate owing to the awareness of a general purpose which has not been excluded. A patient compared the beginning of each analytic hour with the releasing of a compass needle which till then has been held at rest. The magnetic needle does not at once point toward the north, but swings back and forth until it finally takes the proper direction. Here there are two primary possibilities of disturbance: the magnetic needle may not come to rest in a specific direction but keep swinging; or without swinging, it may seem to come to rest too rapidly, too directly, or too exactly. When it does not come to rest, the associations become spread out, the patient talks much, but approaches no unconscious impulse. No common denominator of his remarks shows itself. That is a definite resistance which must be demonstrated as such. It can come about in two ways: *(a)* negatively, through a special fear. (Reich recognized that a constant 'superficiality' of talk, anchored in the character, corresponds to a 'fear of psychic depths' which is identical with a fear of falling, a fear of the depths of one's own body and of one's own excitement.) *(b)* Positively; 'superficial' talk affords a special libidinal gain or an aggressive one (for example, the patient wants to annoy the analyst). If nothing is said for a rather long time either about the neurosis or about daily life, then something is wrong. Often this kind of resistance assumes the form of the patient's not hitting at all upon the idea that those everyday things which really matter must *also* be talked about. Some times a demonstration of 'association' by the analyst is of help here. In certain cases, nothing is said in the analysis about daily life for the reason that daily life is *really* without any interest for the patient. There are persons who live so much in their fantasies that they do not even notice everyday things. In such cases it is our task to make the patient

conscious of the *defense* inherent in such an attitude towards
fantasy and reality, but we must not follow him in such
behavior nor, without paying any attention to reality, fantasy
for example with him about the father's penis in the mother's
body. When the magnetic needle sets itself 'too exactly', the
patient is so filled with the ultimate purpose of the analysis
that he can and will speak only with respect to this purpose,
only 'according to a program'. This form of resistance we see
particularly in compulsion neurotics and other character types
who operate chiefly with the kind of defense called isolation.
They do not succeed in giving their thoughts free play without
control.

We already see how particularly important it is for analysis
to take into consideration the *general* types of defense, since
their effectiveness, if not attacked, *destroys* the value of all
the work otherwise accomplished.

How do our first interventions usually look and what do
we expect from them theoretically? From the very first words
that we pronounce in the analysis we do nothing else than
'demonstrate derivatives as such', and at first the *most superficial ones*. Usually we first endeavor to do away with general
isolations by showing the patient *connections* between events,
feelings, and intentional attitudes, connections which he had
previously not noticed, although they were obvious. (If they
are not so obvious that even the unprepared patient must notice them with 'surprise' as a result of a simple demonstration,
then we will remain silent about them and save their demonstration until later.) Among *ways of behavior* we show *connections* which are calculated first to make the patient *curious*. In
all this, we always strive to demonstrate what we understand by
'psychic reality', with which we wish to work. Furthermore
we demonstrate, whenever it is possible, that the patient in
reality actively brings about things which he seems to experience passively. Moreover, we try to bribe him by showing him,
whenever an opportunity presents itself, how analysis can be
beneficial to him. We shall begin with the demonstration of

the patient's own responsibility in bringing about experiences that seem merely to happen to him.

The patient tries to let himself go completely. Everything now comes 'of itself'. He does not notice that it is he *himself* who interferes with the course of his impulses. The purpose of analysis is *in general* to make the unconscious accessible to the ego, that is, to help the ego to understand that something it has passively experienced is really actively brought about by a part of itself. The aphorism, 'where id was, there shall ego be',[37] means that the ownership of that which happens out of one's own unconscious should be restored to the ego. Applied to symptoms, this notion is certainly incredible to the patient at the beginning of analysis. Therefore, attempts to demonstrate this in relation to the symptoms are contraindicated (we shall talk about 'too deep interpretations' later on). It cannot be emphasized enough that not only conversion symptoms which the patient considers somatogenic, but also the melancholy of a depression (in contrast to ordinary normal sadness), or great anxiety are experienced as *completely alien to the ego,* as things that storm their way over the ego which is itself completely passive in the situation. Thus at the start a 'secret activity' can be demonstrated in what seems to be 'passively experienced', only if we attempt to point out at the most superficial points how the patient is interfering with his own impulses and activities. If we consider once more how instinctual impulses that press towards discharge are in conflict with defensive impulses that prevent the discharge, we see that in analysis we work always and exclusively on the latter, the defensive impulses.

'You are in a state of resistance', is an interpretation which has often been subjected to ridicule. When this interpretation is presented in a tone which attempts to throw upon the patient the responsibility for his difficulties, then it is really ridiculous. But in another tone it is a correct interpretation,

[37] Freud: *New Introductory Lectures on Psychoanalysis.* New York: W. W. Norton and Co., Inc., 1933. p. 112.

and in principle, it seems to me the first correct interpretation to be given. It brings about a change in the patient's attention and makes known to him something about himself that he did not know before. In every conflict of repression the unconscious ego is to be sure unconscious, but nevertheless it is more easily accessible than the warded off instinct. Sometimes 'substituted instinctual impulses' which seem to be more superficially situated become evident first; but these substitute impulses have two aspects, and the defense aspect of their 'substitutive' character is more easily accessible than their nature as representatives of the original unconscious.

Against all this an objection can be raised. The unconscious impulse which pushes toward consciousness and motility is our ally, the defensive ego our enemy. But we are in the situation of a commander whose troops are separated from his allies by the enemy's front. In order to unite our forces with those of our ally, the warded off instinct, we must first break through to him, and for that we need another ally accessible to us, the reasonable ego, which must be detached from the defensive ego. To remain in the metaphor, we must first disintegrate the enemy's ranks with propaganda and win over large portions of his forces.

Premature attempts to reach this ally, the instinct which seeks discharge, must fail. The compulsion neurotic, for example, has regressed to the anal-sadistic level in a flight from the claims of his genital œdipus complex. The question has been asked: should we not in practice gain an advantage from this knowledge of ours and begin at once with the treatment of the actual pathogenic conflict, the genital œdipus complex? An analogous train of thought is apparently followed by all those analysts who expect success from 'bombarding' the patient with 'deep' interpretations, that is, telling as quickly as possible what they themselves have recognized as a pathogenic conflict. This is the case not only with Stekel and his followers, but also with those analysts who, by means of the primal-scene interpretation of a child's game, hope to establish a reasonable ego when none was previously present. 'Contact' with the patient can be brought about in this way under certain circumstances, that is, when this deep interpretation acts as a seduction; but then it can also miscarry like a seduction and evoke reinforced defensive measures. At any rate, in the case of the compulsion neurotic we cannot begin with discussion or treatment of the genital conflicts for the reason that these conflicts are for the time being no longer present, but are replaced by the anal-sadistic conflicts. We cannot begin with the depths without having previously dealt with the surface. And in principle what holds for genitality and anality in the compulsion neurotic holds similarly for instinct and defense against instinct in every analysis.

In a seminar an analyst once described a case whose analysis seemed at a standstill. The patient could no longer speak at all in the analytic hour because he was full of aggressions. The analyst could clearly see that this tendency toward aggression, remaining from childhood in an undischarged form, was now directed against him in the transference. But he could make no progress with it. 'What shall I do?' he asked. For weeks I have been telling him in every hour that he wants to kill me; but he does not accept the interpretation.' Such an interpretation in that sort of situation *augments* the anxiety and with it the ego's defense, instead of diminishing it. The correct interpretation would have been: 'You cannot talk because you are *afraid* that thoughts and impulses might come to you which would be directed against me.'

A still more flagrant case of a similar sort was an analysis that made no progress because of the patient's defense against his aggressive tendencies which had become acute. The analyst reported: 'The patient asks me again and again how long this must go on in this way; since the treatment apparently is making no progress, what can be the result, and the like. I keep telling him that he wants to torment and kill me with these endless questions, but there is no change.' In this case not only has the aggression been interpreted instead of the defense against aggression, but besides this it has been over-

looked that the patient's questions were *actually justified.*
When a treatment costing precious time and money comes
to a standstill, the patient has indeed a right to ask the physician for information about the situation, and not until this
right is admitted and the answer is given can the transference
nature of the patient's affect be demonstrated—and this at first
only from the defense aspect.

In symptoms, in substitute affects and in irrational ways of
behaving, this struggle between a more accessible defense side
and a less accessible instinct side is evident. We see it in all
its stages. Only when it is so far manifest that it can be dis-
closed in conscious and preconscious phenomena can we make
it accessible. Sometimes the defense struggle coming to light
in the analytic material is clearly evident to the patient from
the very beginning; then we can dispense with the 'first act'
of interpretation, the 'isolation from the observing ego'. But
in the face of rigid, affectively shut in, or passively submis-
sive, or generally inelastic persons, there is no sense in talking
about the contents of their defense conflicts; in these cases
the 'isolation' of the defense conflict must precede. In other
cases it is often important, under certain circumstances even
decisive, to recognize that the same struggle which can be
vividly detected by the patient at one point, is effective
also at some other point, where to the patient there appears
to be only an inflexible manner of behavior. In such cases
the same conflict which we can interpret with relative ease
at the point where it is still active, must also, after isolation
from the observing ego, be interpreted in its rigid remainders.

The following case is an example of such a constellation.
A poet, critical of society, being analyzed for oral and anal
character difficulties, has developed in his artistic activity an
original and extremely effective style. His irony is of the type
of a 'stubborn obedience', carried out by taking literally the
utterances and pretexts which he wishes to criticize, and by
means of naïveté and simplicity, exposing deceitful complications. His success with this is particularly impressive in his
antireligious activities. He is to be sure aware of this method

of his through subsequent reflection, but he has no suspicion that in other instances he continually makes use of the same mechanism of 'controversy by means of stubborn obedience' against his own superego; that in situations where he considers himself 'obedient', where he really considers himself 'stupid' in his 'simplicity,' he is unconsciously aggressive and is rebelling against the 'deceitful complexity' of the world of adults. This was already developed when he started in school as a boy of six and had to sit next to a hot iron stove. The heat was so unpleasant that he could not pay attention and merely kept thinking: 'When it's so hot, I can't understand anything'. He never complained in any other way than through this inhibition of learning. He thought that it had to be so hot in school, or else the teacher would not have seated him in that place, and if he could not understand anything, his stupidity was to blame. In the analysis it was necessary that the mechanism which he used actively and consciously for artistic purposes be shown to him also at those points where, unknown to him, it had crystallized in certain characterological ways of behaving.

To 'thaw out' such 'frozen' conflicts between instinct and defense, so that in place of an automatic way of acting a conflict is once more experienced, is indeed a principal task of analysis. For at many points the original pathogenic conflict has led to some chronic ego alteration which takes care of the matter once and for all and spares the individual subsequent more acute types of defense requiring more energy expenditure.

Should our opinion therefore be that every compulsive character must in the course of a psychoanalysis go through acute attacks of anxiety? No. He need not necessarily, I should think, actually experience these anxiety attacks in their full severity; but he need not experience them thus only because correct dosage in analysis can avoid this. In my opinion it is *fundamental* that he really pass through the anxiety which he had previously warded off by means of his compulsive character. But the restoration of mobility at those points where there has been rigidity must not take place with a shock, for analysis also requires *gradualness* of mobilization. Anxiety attacks in the case of former compulsion neurotics can indeed occur in the course of analysis, and they need not be feared. But we are distrustful of too great a preference on the part of analysts for such 'eruptions'. We must not provoke 'breakdowns' and must not, seriously injure the patient's narcissism by continued aping of his characteristics.

With such conditions the Charybdis of too much acting is again approached. There are indeed two opposite types of defense: flight to the theatrical, to magic, to direct libidinal activity (mostly feminine or masochistic); and 'flight to health', away from fantasies to sober reality and finally to words divorced from affects (though later again cathected with affect). When a patient is too 'calm' in analysis, one cannot at first know whether a true lack of affect is present or the suppression of a particularly strong affect. Just as with a dream fragment devoid of affect, one cannot at first tell whether it is relatively insignificant or whether the expression of its significance is merely prevented by a countercathexis. Two locomotives under full steam working against each other with equal power travel just as little as two locomotives not under steam at all. But just as the coal consumption makes clear which of these alternatives is true, so also does the energy consumption reveal the true state of affairs with the patient. Calmness, as defense, fatigues the patient, or its defensive nature can be noted in the rigidity of the musculature or of certain portions of the musculature. For example, a patient may report that his bowel movements are quite in order in such a way that one must take this report as a sign of unsolved anal-erotic conflicts just as much as the report that he is continually constipated or suffers from diarrhœa. In such a case the associations likewise come so characteristically 'in order' that there is no doubt but that they must first be brought into disorder so that later on real order can be attained.

At this point a slight digression may be interposed. Alexander [38] has described as 'neurotic character', a person who is continually impelled by his unsolved childhood conflicts toward unsuitable actions in reality. Alexander asserted that this type of neurotic character can be influenced more successfully by analysis than can a symptomatic neurotic because the latter has regressed from the alloplastic to the autoplastic mode of reaction, and after successful analysis must first acquire the courage which is necessary for progressing to actions in real life. This necessity is absent in the case of the neurotic character who is always acting out anyway. This point of view I should like directly to contradict. The pseudo-alloplastic reactivity of the neurotic character can be changed into a healthy alloplasticity only by being first temporarily transformed into a 'neurotic autoplasticity' and then treated analytically like an ordinary symptom neurosis. Internal conflicts which have been crystallized in spurious object relationships must first be transformed back again to internal conflicts and as such find their solution, before normal object relationships can appear in their place.

What was said above about evacuation of the bowels is also true in regard to sexual potency. The report of a patient that he is capable of complete sexual satisfaction must be sceptically regarded, like the assertion that there exist neuroses with complete orgastic potency, which theoretically there cannot be. Such cases have been repeatedly discussed in detail in case seminars, and every time the relative insufficiency of the orgasm has come to light.

It is relatively easy to find what must be 'thawed out'—what the current analytic task is. It is much more difficult to carry out this task and to find those points where at the moment the system is shaky, where the neurotic defense is weak, and thus the places and times at which the struggle between instinct and defense has remained most alive. This is always a task of

[38] Alexander, Franz: *Der neurotische Charakter*. Int. Ztschr. f. Psa., XIV, 1928. pp. 26–44.

reversing displacements, abolishing isolations, or guiding traces of affect to their proper relationships.

The 'topographical' formula for interpretation was that it should 'make the unconscious conscious'. The correct guessing and naming of the unconscious meanings of a neurotic symptom can sometimes cause its disappearance, but sometimes not. That result depends specifically upon whether such designation of the unconscious meaning succeeds in really altering something dynamically at the point of the instinctual conflict. Therefore the more correct dynamic formula is that we must 'remove the resistances'. Resistance analysis was evolved from interpretation analysis.

That it is not enough to *name* the conflicts becomes particularly clear in a frequently recurring situation: the patient talks, and indeed not without emotion, but with feeling adequate to his really important conflicts; a transference situation for example is being discussed and at the same time there takes place in the way the patient behaves a *duplicate of what is being spoken about, in wordless action on a different level.* How the patient receives the interpretation and reacts to it, what feelings he experiences during the conversation, must then in turn be put into words. If the interpretation of a symptom is especially impressive when it comes about in connection with a new edition of the symptom in the transference, it is quite particularly so when, during the interpretation of the transference phenomenon, the analyst can point out that in the patient's behavior, to which he had given no thought at all, the very same thing is present *once more.*

The possibility of speaking about something without being aware of how real it is, is the basis for a certain type of resistance. There are patients who consciously or unconsciously formulate words without noticing, or indeed with the unconscious purpose of *not* noticing, that behind these words are to be found the *dynamic forces,* which to be sure we can influence only by words. In such a case we must not *talk* with the patient about his conflicts, but should demonstrate to him how he makes use of talking. Other patients try to flee from one instinctual attitude into the opposite one; then again we should not ask which is the more genuine. We should not ask, for example, whether we should 'interpret first the heterosexuality or the homosexuality'. What must be interpreted is *the oscillation between the two positions as defense.*

From the vantage point of this insight into the dynamics of interpretation, several generally known rules can be commented upon here:

(a) 'One should always start the interpretation at the surface.' How otherwise? In what other way could we penetrate to the depths than by beginning at the surface? Analysis must always go on in the layers accessible to the ego at the moment. When an interpretation has no effect, one often asks oneself: 'How could I have interpreted more deeply?' But often the question should more correctly be put: 'How could I have interpreted more superficially?' The deep conflicts also have their representatives in the trifles of everyday life, and it is there that the patient can really become aware of their effectiveness. If the daily trifles do not come to discussion, then a special resistance is present—probably an isolation of the analysis from real life.

(b) 'The patient determines the subject matter of the analytic hour.' This rule is a corollary of that other one, that we must always work with 'living reality'. What does not interest a patient cannot be forced upon him. For example, the premature attempt of little Hans' father to interpret his œdipus complex had to fail, because just then his anal erotism was the subject of the moment.[39] But the word 'interest' requires an explanation. The patient 'determines the subject matter' not always by what he says, but frequently also by what he does *not* talk about, or by *how* he speaks, or what he does. At this point there is very frequently a misunderstanding of the attempt to formulate a 'more systematic technique'. We cannot provide the analyst with a plan of

[39] Freud: *A Phobia in a Five-Year-Old Boy.* Coll. Papers, III. London: Hogarth Press, 1933. p. 207.

procedure applicable to all cases. But we believe that many things not spontaneously put into speech by the patients are shown involuntarily by other indications, and that it is then the task of the analyst to speak about them. That is not 'activity' of any special kind on the part of the analyst, but it is dynamic interpretation. For we must operate at that point where the affect is actually situated at the moment; it must be added that the patient does not know this point and we must first *seek out* the places where the affect is situated.

(c) 'Interpretation of resistance precedes interpretation of content.' This rule again follows automatically from our dynamic insight. An effective interpretation of content succeeds because of a consonance between external auditory perceptions and internally experienced impulses, such a consonance enabling the impulse to break through. A consonance is not possible when it is blocked by a wall of resistance which makes the recognition of the impulse unfeasible. In this case we must first remove the wall. It becomes particularly important to realize this in dealing with long lasting so called 'character resistances'. When a compulsion neurotic does not react to interpretations of content, we cannot console ourselves with Freud's simile,[40] which in other connections is justified, that in the launching of a ship from its moorings one cable at a time has to be released, and the journey does not begin until after the last cable is clear. On the contrary, in analysis in general, it is of prime importance that the cables be released in the *correct sequence,* and first the crucial ones. But this leads us at once into the economic aspects of interpretation.

(d) 'We should avoid too deep and too superficial interpretations.' When is an interpretation too deep? When the patient cannot recognize its correctness by experiencing the impulse in question. When so called too deep interpretations, that is, the naming of unconscious processes which the patient cannot feel within himself, nevertheless show results, such results can be nothing else than 'unspecific' ones; in other

[40] Freud: *The Interpretation of Dreams.* New York: The Macmillan Co., 1923.

words, results that are independent of whether the interpretation is 'correct' and that come about through non-analytic
changes in the dynamics of the patient.[41] They can, for example, be results of a seduction which lies in the fact that what is
otherwise taboo is being spoken about. In favorable cases such
seduction can lead to diminution of anxiety and therewith
to the production of less distorted derivatives; in unfavorable
cases it can lead to aggravation of the fear of instinct and
strengthening of the defense. But even in the most favorable
case such a decrease of anxiety, which rests only on the fact
that the analyst also did something taboo, can last only
as long as the analyst keeps doing this and, as in hypnosis, as
long as the 'rapport' remains unclouded. *By no means* is
such an 'interpretation' an interpretation in the true analytic
sense, which is a real confrontation of the experiencing ego
with something which it had previously warded off.

When is an interpretation 'too superficial'? When, because
of the analyst's fear of affects, it in some way plays along with
the patient's efforts to cover up his affects. Especially the
neglect of sufficiently definite transference interpretations can
bring a bitter retribution. While a transference is developing,
there are present much clearer and more easily recognized
derivatives of the true context to which the transference
behavior belongs; when a more 'intensive' transference has
developed and there is a closer interweaving of the impulses
with the person of the analyst, the real context to which these
impulses belong has become less recognizable to the patient.
We cannot evade resistances; he who wishes to operate has to
cut and must not be afraid of blood. By the omission of
mature interpretations at least as much can be spoiled as by
the presenting of immature ones.

The paradoxical rule that the analyst should drop an interpretation which the patient accepts and insist upon one which
he rejects sounds ingenious, but it is certainly fundamentally
wrong. Of course there is a way of apparently accepting inter-

[41] *Cf.* Glover, Edward: *The Therapeutic Effect of Inexact Interpretation.*
Int. J. Psa., XII, 1931. pp. 397-411.

pretations which is resistance, but a real assent of the patient is our goal. And of course there is a way of 'refusing' interpretations with words, and still the behavior or following associations betray that the interpretations were nevertheless accepted. A true 'no' on the part of the patient is a proof that the interpretation was wrong, and if not wrong in content, then not presented correctly from the point of view of dynamics or economics.

In addition to the dynamics, the economics of interpretation must also be discussed. We must work not only at the point of actual instinctual conflicts, but at the point of the *most important* current instinctual conflicts. It is the point of the most important conflicts *at the moment.* For this reason the *sequence* in which the interpretations are presented is of such great importance.

In the psychic realm, as is well known, overdetermination is the rule: in every psychic act every unconscious tendency is represented. Therefore it is of concern to the analyst which of the unconscious tendencies he should pick out. That is what Rado meant when he used to say, 'Interpretation is an economic process'. The correctness of this view in practice has been made clear to us especially by Reich [42] in his writings on technique. There is no doubt that through interpretation incorrect in the economic sense, we are threatened with 'chaotic situations'. However, we must not forget two things: *(1)* not all 'chaotic situations' need be the results of faulty analysis. Spontaneous 'chaotic situations' also exist; for example, there are certain character disturbances which are marked by the disorder and unreliability of their extremely ambivalent object relationships and by the alternating appearance of instinctual tendencies and defensive attitudes from all possible stages of development. These disturbances could not be otherwise diagnosed than as 'spontaneous chaotic situations', and are mostly ego disturbances of traumatic origin. *(2)* An enormous rôle is played in the psychological domain

[42] Reich, Wilhelm: *Charakteranalyse.* Vienna, 1933 (published by the author).

by something similar to what is known in geology as 'faulting'. Current imponderables of life which represent now an instinct temptation, now a reinforcement of anxiety, keep bringing about at each moment varying displacements of the 'psychic layers'. Interpretation takes place *not* exactly in reversed historical sequence. Nevertheless the sequence of the interpretations remains economically determined; otherwise, interpretations presented in an arbitrary order result in arbitrary, that is, irregular dynamic alterations: instinct becomes defense, defense becomes instinct, and we have a confusion of everything.

My meaning will perhaps become clearer through another metaphor: one cannot see the forest for the trees. In case seminars we often hear correct interpretations of details, but the inexperienced analyst does not know what the situation of the entire person is—just which of his observations is 'important', because it returns in various forms and reflects a structure; and what, on the other hand, is 'unimportant', because it is the chance formation of a libidinal situation of the moment.

Freud [43] once warned us against attempting too often in the course of an analysis to sketch a picture of the case. We must always be ready to let ourselves be led by the patient to something quite different from what we had expected. However, we can also go too far in condemning the formulation of case summaries during treatment. In my opinion such case formulations can be of two types: one which at the beginning helps tremendously, is indeed necessary, and one which is harmful. Specifically, the analyst can make use of the symptomatology, impression of the personality, behavior and also childhood memories in order to formulate for himself a dynamic and economic collective picture of the structure of the case, merely an orientation system out of which further problems then follow. That type of formulation is *necessary*. With such a framework the analyst listens further with freely floating attention, and with it he orients himself in that oscillation to intelligent understanding previously described.

[43] Freud: *Recommendations for Physicians on the Psycho-Analytic Method of Treatment.* Coll. Papers, II. pp. 326–327.

Of course the framework is altered according to new experiences but, since it is merely a *framework*, by and large it remains standing and becomes gradually more definite. It contains genetic elements, too, because we always experience a psychic structure as a precipitate of its developmental history. However, it does *not* include the constructions of details of infantile events deduced from the first screen memories. It is such constructions, necessary in their own good time, which constitute the other, hindering type of case formulations, and this type is often set up because of a worry of the analyst that he 'does not understand the case'. But if an analyst does not understand the details of his patient's childhood from the beginning, that is nothing to worry about. We really need not trouble ourselves so actively about the patient's childhood. It is still actively present anyhow in the behavior of the patient today; otherwise it would not interest us at all. If only we put the present in order correctly and understand it, we shall thereby make new impulses possible for the patient, until the childhood material comes of itself.

On the economic side belongs the *dosage* of interpretations. It is a task of the physician to have the therapeutic process involve as little pain to the patient as is possible. In particular, the 'shattering of a narcissistic armor' is painful. We shall return to the subject of 'gradualness' in the discussion of 'working through'.

Alexander [44] expressed the opinion recently that resistances should, if possible, be attacked only by the naming of that against which they are directed. This technique cannot always be correct. To be sure, defense and instinct are in fact so bound up with each other that we sometimes cannot name one without at the same time working on the other. However, such a designation of what is warded off is indeed frequently 'nonsense', because the patient cannot find in himself what has been designated, as long as a resistance prevents its reaching the preconscious. It would be just as nonsensical in such a situation to leave the resistance untreated because

44 Alexander, Franz: *The Problems of Psychoanalytic Technique.* The Psa. Quarterly, IV, 1935 p. 600.

then nothing at all would ever be changed. Even if nothing else can be said about a resistance than that it is present, it is certainly better to call the patient's attention to it than to leave it unheeded.

The more one knows about the nature, origin, and purpose of a resistance, the better can he understand its acute occurrence and demonstrate it to the patient. Therefore the more *factual* material one knows about the patient, the more easily an analysis is carried out; also, only the knowledge of his history enables us to understand the allusions contained in his associations. Especially in the beginning of an analysis, it is an important task of the analyst to *accumulate* as much factual material as possible from the life of the patient. Perhaps, since my aim is to formulate a theory of technique, I have entered too hurriedly into the dynamics and economics of interpretation, and have therefore neglected to talk about the necessity for the preceding accumulation of material. Every bit of knowledge concerning the past facilitates for us the understanding of the present. As long as a patient tells us facts about his past, we shall gratefully accept them—unless, as sometimes occurs, a particular contraindication is present, when such talking about the past represents a resistance aiming to prevent us from working with 'living material'.

What has been said about the dynamics and economics of interpretation in general, applies of course also to dream interpretation. Dream interpretations that are incorrect from the economic standpoint are not only not accepted, but they make the analysis difficult or spoil it for later on because through such interpretations the patient gets a premature intellectual familiarity with the ideational content of his unconscious, and the analyst is then in the position of one who has shot off his ammunition before it was possible to hit the mark.

Should dream interpretations be therefore completely avoided as long as the character resistances have not been dissolved? Sometimes that is correct. There are some particular contraindications to dream interpretations: *(1)* The *isolation* of 'deep' dreams by a more superficial resistance. The dreams deal with very deep lying conflicts of the patient, of which he cannot yet feel the faintest derivatives in his waking life ('dreams of the unsuspecting'). (2) Dream interpretation has taken on too much of a certain transference significance. As an activity it signifies in itself a special libidinal satisfaction for the patient or allays a special anxiety. In this case the unconscious significance of dream interpretation must first be recognized and eliminated, before it can be practiced. But apart from such special contraindications there is, in my opinion, no reason not to utilize the 'royal road to the unconscious' as much as possible.

We will remember that Freud [45] said that in the use of dream interpretation in practical analysis, two activities must be differentiated: the translation of the manifest dream into the latent dream thoughts, and the utilization for the analysis of what has been found out through the translation. Now it is certainly correct that in this second activity we must let ourselves be governed by the caution which insight into the economic aspect of interpretation prescribes for us. However, one often cannot perform the act of translating beyond a certain point without communicating to the patient what has already been guessed, and this communication is in itself an 'interpretation'. The two phases of interpretation cannot be strictly separated from each other in practice, and an exaggerated choice by the analyst of what should be interpreted is thus impossible. Another circumstance excludes such a possibility. In free association, associations often become understandable through what *follows*. Therefore before this subsequent association has been given, one cannot know what to omit from an interpretation.

Especially for the understanding of the immediate preconscious situation, dreams can often be amply utilized. Another question is how far it is possible to utilize for analysis manifest dream texts even without dream analysis. The observation of peculiarities of character and types of defense by the manner in which the distortion takes place in dreams is an important field of investigation and one that is certainly too

[45] Freud: *Bemerkungen zur Theorie und Praxis der Traumdeutung* (1923) Ges. Schr., III. pp. 308–309.

little cultivated as yet. How characteristic, for example, of a person whose nature is marked by a 'flight into reality', is the enormous development of 'secondary elaboration' in his dreams, which at every point produces intelligible connections. Also important in the course of the analysis as a mirror for the changing state of the economic equilibrium between instincts and instinct defenses, is the changing of the mechanisms of distortion in the manifest dream content.[46] On the other hand, I am for various reasons very sceptical of attempts to classify the manifest dreams according to the prevailing instinct groups, to count the representatives in the individual groups and thus to draw graphs.

Should we say that the analyst must always know what he is doing, why he interprets, and what he expects each time from his activity? I should like especially not to be misunderstood in this, for I do not mean to say that we should replace intuition and freely floating attention with exertion of the intellect. What is meant is that, after we have reflected upon it, we should always be able to explain what we are doing, why we interpret, and what we expect each time from our activity.

In conclusion: *how does interpretation work?* We do not want to differentiate at this point between interpretations of resistance and interpretations of instinct, but to ask about the factors common to both. The answer in general is this: the attention of the ego is drawn to a 'preconscious derivative'. How does that take place? *(1)* What is to be interpreted is first *isolated* from the experiencing part of the ego. This preliminary task drops out when the patient already has some critical attitude towards that which is to be interpreted. *(2)* The patient's attention is drawn to his own *activity: he himself* has been bringing about that which up to now he has thought he was experiencing passively. *(3)* He comprehends that he had motives for this activity which hitherto he did not know of. *(4)* He comes to note that *at*

---

[46] Cf. French, Thomas M.: *A Clinical Study of Learning in the Course of a Psychoanalytic Treatment.* The Psa. Quarterly, V, 1936. pp. 148–194.

some other point, too, he harbors something similar, or something that is in some way associatively connected. *(5)* With the help of these observations he becomes able to produce less distorted 'derivatives', and through these the *origin* of his behavior gradually becomes clear.

Why does a patient 'accept' interpretations? *(1)* Because he recognizes as true within himself that which has been interpreted to him. We interpret, as is well known, what is already in the preconscious—and just a *little bit more*—which thereby becomes capable of entering consciousness. *(2)* As a result of the paradoxically designated 'rational transference', that is, because of a positive emotional attitude towards the analyst which induces the patient to take a less sceptical view concerning anything expressed by the analyst. *(3)* As a result of identification with the interpreting analyst. Doubtless the patient essentially imitates the analyst when he now divides his ego into an observing and an experiencing portion and so comes to see the discrepancy between his impulses, determined by his past, and his present reality.

In this section of our discussion about psychoanalytic technique we have attempted, through working out the dynamics and economics of interpretation, to make more concrete what we had set forth in the previous section concerning the essential mode of action of interpretations in general. The abundance of the material to be dealt with caused the discussion to become somewhat tangled. Perhaps before we proceed further we should make what has been said still more concrete and thus again draw the thread of our logic taut. I propose to do this by two means: first, by supplementing from the structural side what has been said concerning dynamics and economics through extending our inquiry to the question of so called ego analysis and id analysis; second, by investigating in particular that special case of interpretation which directly constitutes a criterion of analysis: the handling of the transference.

IV

Structural Aspects of Interpretation

The subject matter of the previous section of our discussion dealt with what takes place in psychoanalytic interpretation: the interference in the play of psychic forces (dynamics) and the alteration of the distribution of psychic energy (economics). We can best elucidate what has been said if we now begin with a third point of view, the *structural*. To what extent does the interpreting analyst work upon the ego, and to what extent upon the id and the superego?

In a direct sense the analyst works *exclusively* upon the *ego*. We need only to think of the definition of the ego: as soon as an ego exists at all, through it every influence of the environment upon the psyche takes place; the understanding of the meaning of words is particularly a concern of the ego. To be sure, the id can also be changed by experience. Fixations, in so far as they are conditioned by particular satisfactions or privations, are alterations in the domain of the id brought about by experience. Likewise regressions, although we call them 'defenses', give the impression of a general tendency of the id in the case of loss of satisfactions, to reach back to situations where things were otherwise. We speak of 'instinct structures', that is, id formations which come about through the alternate action of satisfactions and deprivations. But all these influences of the environment upon the id always take place *indirectly* by way of the ego. If the ego did not undertake instinctual activities, no instinctual tendency could be canalized in the id; if the ego did not set up defenses, the id would remain unaltered. When through analytic treatment we make possible genital primacy, that is certainly an alteration of the id; but it comes about through influencing the ego.

However, one could express the view that we nevertheless appeal to the id with our interpretations, for there are no sharp boundaries between ego and id (except at those points where barriers have been created by countercathexes). There exist archaic types of movements and perceptions very close to the id, related to identifications, diffuse, undifferentiated, and unconscious. In this connection the following comparison is illuminating: although there exist in multicellular organisms, respiratory and digestive organs specially differentiated for the functions of respiration and digestion, these are primary functions of all living matter; and before the evolution of respiratory and digestive organs, and to a certain extent even after this evolution, every living cell breathes and digests in a less differentiated way. Now in the same sense motility and perception, in other words dealing with the environment, are the primary functions of all psychic substance; and before there existed an ego, an organ specially differentiated for these tasks, they were carried out by the totality of the psychic substance.

Could and should we not with our interpretations reach these early id-related layers and not the ego? Of course it sometimes happens that they are reached. Such is the case most clearly in *hypnosis* in which the upper ego layers are artificially abolished in order to reëstablish the primitive ego functions, or in order that ego functions may be projected. (The hypnotist not only takes over the functions of the superego of the subject but can be considered also as a 'parasitical double' of the ego itself.) Indeed we make use of 'suggestion' in analysis too, especially in the battle against the resistances. But when we attempt thus to eliminate the ego, or more correctly the upper layers of the ego, a danger arises. For the maintenance of this projection, an attachment to the object-person is needed; success cannot be depended upon (as in the case of every transference success), and when later an analysis of the transference follows, the success is demolished. Only a subsequent demonstration directed to the upper layers of the ego, in the form of a 'working through' of what has emerged in catharsis-like eruptions, can bring about the previously discussed confrontation of the past and the present, free from magic. For this purpose we must direct our attention to the higher layers of the ego and that is what the analyst does. There sometimes arises the problem, as we have said before, of what is to be done when there is an insufficiency of the ego. In such cases the task is to utilize the healthy remnants of the ego, in order gradually to enlarge it to proportions suitable for the analytic work and to try variations in analytic technique suited to the ego remnants; or finally, to attempt a preanalytic pedagogical period of training of the individual.

Let us consider once more the basic conflict. Something against which the ego is defending itself wishes to break through to consciousness and motility, and the resistance corresponds essentially to the defensive forces of the ego. These we try to dissolve. The id impulse we do not need to strengthen and indeed we cannot do so. Neither making conscious an unconscious impulse by naming it, nor 'seduction' is effective to strengthen the instincts. For example when a countercathexis has been so far broken down by analysis that a previously tabooed instinctual gratification would be possible and a new experience acts as a seduction, we must understand that this 'seduction' represents merely a weakening of the resistance through the experience of a satisfaction which comes to the aid of analysis.

In fine, it may then be said that we can take either the defending forces or what is being defended against as the subject of our discussions in analysis, but both types of discussion operate upon the ego and only indirectly upon the id or the superego.

When we have recognized that all analysis is really ego analysis, we can consider the expressions 'ego analysis' and 'id analysis' in a narrower sense that justifies their use. We may then ask when and how we make the defending forces (ego) and when and how we make the object of the defense (id) the subject of analytic interpretations. We then realize that we have already made a number of things clear concerning this matter. Recall, for example, the instance in which the interpretation, 'You are aggressive', was incorrectly given for, 'You are afraid that you might be aggressive'. We formulated the general rule: interpretation of resistance precedes interpretation of content.

Sometimes, to be sure, it is not defensive attitudes themselves but substitutive instinctual impulses pervading them that are directly experienced, among others those that are involved in symptoms. In this case we find that these phenomena have *two sides,* and of the two the defensive side is the more accessible. By no means is a given phenomenon always *either* defense and in the ego, *or* instinct and in the id. *Derivatives* always comprise *both;* instinct serves for suppression of instinct. A passive instinctual longing can be reinforced to suppress an active one, and the like. Phenomena such as the overcompensation of an impulse by means of an opposite impulse (for example, overcompensatory replacement of hate by love) show this most clearly. The problem may be rather more complicated, in that there are not only two, but three (or more) 'psychic layers': instinct—defense—superficial instinctual attitude. When we interpret we must be quite clear whether an experienced instinctual impulse is original, has passed through a defense, or serves directly defensive purposes.

In instances of 'return of the repressed', the repressed impulse has changed its character; it has become alien to the ego and though it is regarded as an instinct, it is not felt in the same direct way as originally. When a patient has a dream of incest at the beginning of an analysis, it is clear to the analyst that the instinctual impulse corresponding to the manifest dream content is active in the patient; but this is not felt to be true by the patient. If he be told that he really wishes to consummate the incestuous act he dreamed about, he will not know what to make of it. He can much more easily be led to discover in himself other attitudes which are more superficial but about which also at first he does not know. Very different attitudes may be involved—attitudes such as, 'If I admit this, the analyst will leave me in peace' (in one respect or another); or attitudes of obligingness in the transference or, on the contrary, of ridicule. In the example of the incestuous dream *both* are contained, the attitude of obligingness or ridicule towards the analyst as well as the incestuous wish, but in *different layers*. The one is nearer the ego and has to be interpreted first.

Fixations present a similar problem. They are seldom determined by a simple desire for the repetition of such instinctual activities as at one time have found special satisfaction or frustration. Mostly they seek instinctual gratifications that are at the same time suitable for dispelling an opposing anxiety. The striving to dispel anxiety and the striving for instinctual satisfaction are then situated on *different levels*.

The fact that obvious instinctual attitudes in reality may serve defense purposes or may be the expression of quite different hidden instincts, becomes particularly clear in phenomena of 'pseudo-sexuality'. Groddeck, who had a predilection for paradoxes, once said in praise of the omnipotence of the erotic: 'A glance, a touch of the hand can be the highest point in a human life. It is not true that sexual intercourse represents the culmination of erotic life. People are really bored with it!' We believe that such an evaluation can hold true only for sexually deranged persons, but we must inquire further why these persons practise the tiresome sexual intercourse nevertheless. If the reply is, 'Because it is customary', that is merely a paraphrase for, 'Because I wish to satisfy a narcissistic need not to be different from others'. We recognize, however, that only in the rarest instances will that be the most essential motive; it is far more important that in carrying out the sexual act a whole series of the most varied other *narcissistic needs* be satisfied.

The sexual fantasies and lies of a woman patient, for example, had essentially the function of denying certain sexual experiences of her early childhood and thus served primarily as defense, and she made the same use of masturbation accompanied by fantasies. It was found that there was a break in the history of her masturbation. After an experience that

mobilized the anxiety of the primal scene she had stopped mas-
turbating, and then after several years had resumed it again
most intensively as a sort of compulsive masturbation of a quite
different character. Analysis showed that this new masturbation was a defensive measure. She wished primarily to convince herself of the following: 'I am not afraid of my own body,
for it really gives me pleasure'. We very frequently meet such
attempts to cry down an anxiety, which opposes sexual activity
by means of actual sexual activities which then cannot be
enjoyed in a normal way. Thus masturbation and also sexual
intercourse can serve as *defense against anxiety*. By the per-
formance of acts which apparently have a sexual character, these
patients succeed in repressing their true sexual impulses.

Of course the normal sexual instincts themselves are always
also contained in such 'pseudo-sexuality'. A phenomenon of
threefold stratification results. Sensations which would correspond to original instinctual impulses can still send no
derivatives into consciousness; the defense function is closer
to the ego and must be interpreted first. To be sure, we must
in this connection be clear concerning the relationship between
the concepts of 'satisfaction of instinct' and 'defense against
instinct'. It will not do to call instinctual satisfaction a
'defense against instinct', as Nunberg [47] does, on the ground
that the satisfaction puts an end to unpleasant instinctual
tension. When there is no expenditure of countercathexis,
there is no sense in speaking of 'defense'. Similarly, when a
normal child progresses in its development from anal eroticism
to genitality, so that his anal desires are gone, we should not
say that he has repressed his anal eroticism by means of his
genitality.

In a certain sense the infantile sexuality of the neurotic
always has defensive character as well, in so far as it is also a
consequence of the anxiety which caused it to take the place
of adult genital sexuality. This is particularly clear, for

[47] Nunberg, Hermann: *Allgemeine Neurosenlehre auf psychoanalytischer Grundlage*. Berne and Berlin: Verlag Hans Huber, 1932. p. 198.

example, in the *perversions,* in which the instinctual character
and capability for enjoyment are retained in contrast to the
'pseudo-potency' of the compulsion neurotic.   Perversions are
measures for dispelling an anxiety which is opposed to sexual
enjoyment, and these measures do afford a relative enjoyment
because they use a partial instinct suitable for dispelling
anxiety.   One thinks of another example of threefold stratification in the 'return of repressed sadism' in the case of overly
kind persons who torment others by their excessive kindness.
What we term 'defensive attitude' always has an instinctual side
to it as well.   The manner in which a compulsion neurotic
isolates always contains the isolated factor too; but the isolating
function is closer to his ego.

Let us now consider a theory of Alexander [48] which I wish
to contradict in order to make these points still clearer.   It is
his opinion that there are two types of neuroses: the first are
those based on a conflict between an instinct and a defensive
impulse of the ego, for example between a masculine œdipus
wish and a fear of being castrated for it; the second are neuroses based on conflicts between two instincts, for example
between a masculine œdipus wish and a passive feminine
desire to be castrated.   We have doubts however about the
'conflict between two instincts'.   It is the essence of the id
that there are no contradictions in it.   Instincts antagonistic
in content can be satisfied successively or in derivatives common
to both (for instance, representation by means of the opposite).
To be sure, neuroses of the second type *exist,* but the instinctual conflict underlying them is always a *structural* conflict
as well.   One of the contradictory instincts is situated at
the moment closer to the ego, is maintained as an ego defense
and reinforced for the defensive purposes of the ego; it is,
although instinctual in nature, in a relative sense a defense
against instinct, in comparison with deeper, warded off instincts.
We need to have a sufficiently vivid conception of the dynamics
of the psyche.   It is not that a single instinct is in a struggle

[48] Alexander, Franz: *The Relation of Structural and Instinctual Conflicts.*
The Psa. Quarterly, II, 1933. pp. 181–207.

against a defensive impulse; there are always many instincts, many defensive impulses, a living struggle, a mutual interpenetration. Very seldom does a defensive activity bring a conflict to a final standstill. Almost always there is both a breaking through of the warded off instincts in the defensive activity itself, and a further defense against the defensive actions themselves, permeated as they are with instinctual elements. There are reaction-formations against reaction-formations. There exists not only the 'three-fold stratification' of *(1)* instinct *(2)* defense *(3)* resurgence of instinct, but also of *(1)* instinct *(2)* defense *(3)* defense against defense—as when a man passively feminine, because of castration anxiety overcompensates and assumes an exaggerated masculine bearing.

Conspicuous examples for the rule that 'interpretation begins on the defense side' are what we may call the 'reversed transference interpretation' and also the 'reversed sexual interpretation'. The 'transference interpretation' says schematically: 'It is not I towards whom your feelings are directed; you really mean your father'. Nowadays there are many patients who, knowing about transference, defend themselves against emerging instinctual excitement by referring to its transference significance. In such instances the 'reversed transference interpretation' is: 'You are not aroused at this moment about your father, but about me'. Not until the patient is convinced of this, can the origin of his emotion be discussed. The 'sexual interpretation' says schematically: 'This non-sexual action has actually a sexual character'. In the case of 'pseudo-sexuality' the 'reversed sexual interpretation' must come first as follows: 'This sexual action or this confession of sexuality is not genuine; it is a defense, an expression of your fear of instincts'.

The contrast between instinct and defense against instinct is thus a relative one. Genetically the energy for defense against instinct is always instinctual energy. The environment and the ego as a representative of the environment alter the character and direction of many instinct components in the course of development. Then they may retransform further what was previously altered, and in this manner stratification comes about. Approximately and in the rough, the order of the interpretations, that is the order in which the layers become demonstrable, must therefore correspond to the historical order in reverse, the latest coming first, the earliest last. We mentioned before that this pattern is distorted in practice by the 'faulting' that comes about in accordance with opportunities for gratification or with increase and decrease of anxiety in the experiences of everyday life. The occasional appearance of such 'faulting' during a treatment should be recognized. When for example in dream or in behavior there is a preponderance first of one, then of the other of the forces that are in conflict with one another, momentary decisions need by no means be final ones and we must therefore be cautious in making prognoses from dreams. To be sure, at other times the layers are really broken through in the course of the analysis, and this too is shown in alterations of behavior and of dreams. Such a change is then permanent and embraces to a certain degree the entire material of the analysis. How even then there may still be relapses, we shall discuss under the heading of 'working through'.

The contrast between ego and id is a sharp one only where a countercathexis is present; otherwise the two domains shade into each other. 'Derivatives' were compared by Freud [49] with 'human half-breeds'. In a certain sense it can be said that all defense is 'relative defense'; relative to one layer it is defense, and at the same time, relative to another layer it is that which is warded off. There exists in the human psyche a particularly impressive example of this: the superego whose demands, analogous to instincts, are warded off, is in essence itself a defense structure. Thus the rule, 'interpretation of defense precedes id interpretation', does not always mean that one content should be taken up in discussion, another not; more often it means that certain characteristics or connections of a given content should be discussed sooner than others.

The 'interpretation of defense' has certain characteristics

[49] Freud: *The Unconscious.* Coll. Papers, IV. London: Hogarth Press, 1934. p. 123.

in common with 'id interpretation': in the one as well as in the other something is demonstrated that the ego does not see and does not wish to see, but is able to observe after a shift of attention; in the case of the one as well as of the other, with every remobilization of the conflict there are relapses and the necessity of 'working through'; for both types of interpretation the task is to establish the historical foundations of the attitude in question, to reduce the phenomenon to past occasions for which it was appropriate. Now let us consider certain factors specific for 'ego analysis'.

The sexuality of the neurotic it was discovered, had been transformed because of anxiety into infantile sexuality which did not appear directly but which the analyst had to know about in order to unmask its substitutes. Psychoanalysis therefore had first to investigate this infantile sexuality, to be able to point it out so that the repressed impulses might be readmitted into the ego. This was an important task with which psychoanalysis was long occupied. The inadequacy of the formula, 'to make the unconscious conscious', the theoretical recognition that it was a matter of eliminating resistances, led then to the question whether that could not better be accomplished directly through studying the resistances and making them conscious.

At this point a theoretical digression that I shall only intimate would be in place. With the study of resistances the contrast between psychoanalysis and psychology diminished. While psychology had as its essential aim the description and understanding of the manifest psychic behavior of an individual, psychoanalysis sought to investigate the *general* laws of human psychic life. The instincts, studied first, were relatively the same for all individuals. When psychoanalysis now turns its attention to studies of the ego too, it starts to study the differences between individuals and approaches the subject matter of general psychology. But in this study psychoanalysis differs from psychology because knowing the instincts from which the ego originates through alterations of them by the environment, it can therefore understand the ego differences among human beings from a causal and genetic viewpoint.

It is important to state something else at this point. So far
we have used the expressions 'defense' and 'defense against
instinct' synonymously. There exist however defenses against
every kind of displeasure, against unpleasant perceptions as
well as unpleasant affects, and especially against anxiety. We
know that anxiety is in the first place something that the ego
experiences when a certain excessive amount of excitation
floods the id; later, it is something that the ego uses for the
development of defenses against instinct, a *motive* for defense
when the ego arrives at the judgment that such a flooding might
ensue. If this 'domestication' of anxiety into an 'anxiety
signal' succeeds, such an institution might be extremely welcome to an ego oriented according to the reality principle. But
the purposive arrangement of an anxiety signal often miscarries:
the ego's judgment of the existence of a situation which could
become a traumatic one, actually causes the occurrence of this
traumatic situation. The attempt to give a warning signal of
anxiety acts like a lighted match in a powder barrel because of
a damming up of libido that is already present. Only this
circumstance is responsible for the application of the powerful
quantities of countercathexis in the defense against anxiety that
one often observes. There exist defensive attitudes directed
not against the situation in which anxiety might arise but only
against the appearance of the anxiety *affect* itself. Practically,
to be sure, defense against anxiety and defense against instinct
frequently coincide, since the pathogenic avoidances of instinct
always take place with the purpose of avoiding the anxiety that
is bound up with the instinct; moreover there exist avoidances
of anxiety anchored in the character which, independent of the
condition of the individual's own instincts, seek to evade only
external sources of anxiety. For a psychoanalytic charac-
terology these 'defenses against anxiety', as contrasted with
'defenses against instinct', are of importance.

Interpretation of individual defense mechanisms presents the
same difficulties that are encountered in the interpretation of
instincts: many things are present at the same time, and only
the *relative proportions* decide what is *significant* in a given

situation. Defense mechanisms particularly should be attacked correctly from the *economic* point of view in interpretation. Examples of their confused interrelationships are offered by every compulsion neurosis:

(1) Every compulsion neurosis has warded off objectionable instinctual impulses first by regression to the anal-sadistic level of the libido; in so far as it is a compulsion neurosis however, and not a coprophilia, it has then further warded off with other methods the instinctual impulses that appeared because of the regression.

(2) Every compulsion neurosis isolates from one another things that belong together but then applies other measures, for example repression, against some of the isolated material.

(3) It is characteristic of compulsion neurosis that the symptoms which serve for defense are always secondarily sexualized, and then must be warded off in their turn. Repeating and counting compulsions offer us good instances of this. Their unconscious meaning is that the act which is to be 'undone' through repetition (in which then the continued repetition can be replaced by simply counting) is supposed to be carried out in isolation from the opposing instinctual impulse; but since this impulse penetrates the defensive repetition, the warding off attitude must be warded off again by a new repetition.

The correct application of the economic criteria of interpretation in the analysis of defense mechanisms is still more important in the case of neurotic characters. These are egos restricted by defensive measures, egos which waste energy through constant countercathexes and lose certain gradations of character through renunciations because they respond to external stimuli only with definite patterns, thus sacrificing liveness and elasticity. By means of these distortions, after-repressions are spared and more acute and fearful conflicts are avoided by recourse to renunciations that take place and become chronic. In this manner the ego-restricting ways of behavior with their aim of anchoring the defense against instinct are not experienced as symptoms alien to the ego but are elaborated into the ego itself; their chronic activity prevents instinct from becoming manifest, so that instead of a living conflict between instinct and defense, we see something rigid which to the patient himself does not—or at least not always—present any problem. The relative constancy of the defensive attitude in the face of various environmental tasks or instinctual contents is a special problem. We do not wish to pursue this topic further in this study devoted to psychoanalytic technique.

Since we cannot in practice attack any possible constitutional factors, our aim remains to analyze *historically* the defensive attitudes as thoroughly as possible, so that through their analysis the *history of the instinctual conflicts* of the individual is made clear to us. This is accomplished through two lines of procedure: *(a)* by determining the relationship of defensive attitudes to instinct fixations; *(b)* by finding either the historical situations in which the defensive attitudes were relatively appropriate in certain episodes of life in the past, or the manner and means by which the environment has forced upon the individual just this method of defense. The last may have occurred through circumstances which blocked all other possibilities, or through the behavior of persons with whom the individual identified himself.

Three questions now present themselves: *(1)* the question of the relationship of 'character' in general to 'defense' *(2)* the relationship between 'character defense' and other types of defense, and *(3)* the question of 'defense transference'.

The first question does not belong to the problems of psychoanalytic technique. We wish only to remark about it that the concept of 'character' evidently has a broader compass than the 'modes of defense anchored in the character' which we have here discussed. The organized grouping of the instinctual energies, the manner in which the ego behaves in its instinctual activities, the habitual way the ego unites various tasks with one another in order to give them a common solution, all this too belongs to the 'character'. For analytic *practice* the defense aspect of the character has by far the most outstanding significance.

The second question about the relationship between character defense and other types of defense is an important one for technique. The defensive attitudes of an individual can be divided into occasional and habitual ones. The habitual ones can then be further subdivided. There are persons who assume a certain defensive attitude only in certain situations (external or internal situations involving the mobilization of certain instincts), and other persons who persist in a defensive attitude and thus act as if there were continually present instinctual temptations that need to be warded off. Such persons are for defensive purposes impudent or polite, empty of affect or always proving that it is another person's fault; *always* and *unspecifically* and with reference to all or to nearly all people. Such attitudes may be designated 'character defenses' in a narrower sense in contrast to other modes of defense. We have already said that where this type of defense prevails, it is particularly urgent that we work *first* to release the personality from its rigidity because it is in this that the pathogenic energies are really bound. Frequently even in cases in which a living struggle between instinct and defense appears at other places, the directing of one's attention to the 'rigid' defenses can be of decisive importance.

Patients with character defenses show their character attitudes towards the analyst too. Should this be called a 'transference' manifestation? The answer is yes if transference is defined to mean that attitudes originating in other earlier situations are repeated in the analysand's behavior towards the analyst. If transference is defined as the patient's misunderstanding of the present in terms of the past, the question is still to be answered affirmatively. Here however are observed in the relations to the analyst, unspecific reactions which change in changing situations. The attitude is not specific for the analytic situation. The attitude in question is rigid, general, unspecific, and can therefore be contrasted to a 'transference situation' in the narrower sense, in which the patient reacts to the analyst in a mobile and specific manner, in the same way as at one time in the past he reacted or wished to react to a certain definite person.

Upon what does it depend that one patient produces more of the living 'transference resistance', another more of the 'rigid character resistance'? Does perhaps the latter originate in an earlier period of development when to an ego capable only of partial object relationships the person reacted to was still indifferent? Does the distinction reside in the contrast that in the former case true object relationships are present, while in the latter the persons of the environment are merely means for alleviating intrapsychic conflicts? A more probable assumption is that the difference depends upon whether an instinctual conflict has diffused from its original localization into all of the rest of the individual's life, or whether it became isolated. It depends, in other words, upon whether the ego banishes anxiety and symptoms from its domain after their first appearance by some further defensive measure (the 'transference action' would then be in the escape-discharge), or whether the ego builds the anxiety and symptom into itself, altering its own character. The technically valid rule is that in order to attack them successfully, we must *first change character resistances into transference resistances* exactly in the same well-known way that we, as previously discussed, first change character neuroses into symptomatic neuroses.

Concerning the third question, 'defense transference', the task of analysis as in the 'analysis of defenses' must remain the reduction of the phenomena to their historical basis. The so called 'defense transference' depends upon two things: *(1)* the general human inclination to adjust actions according to previous experiences; to retain as long as possible something which once proved effective, and when a danger returns, to make use of the same means that once afforded aid against a similar danger—while in the meantime changes have ensued which make unsuitable in the present what at an earlier time was appropriate. Why something, which in earlier life was a danger situation fitting to the moment, is retained long after it has ceased to be real, remains a problem. The answer to this problem may be found in the consideration that because the defensive action was mobilized so early in life, the entire conflict was withdrawn from the reasonable ego, and judgment concerning just that type of danger did not take part in the subsequent development of the total per- sonality. *(2)* The individual wishes to 'transfer his instincts'. He strives again and again for satisfactions but again and again the ego responds to this striving with the memory of those factors which at a former time caused anxiety. The extremely displeasurable repetition of the 'passing of the œdipus complex' in the analytic transference,[50] seems to me to be only relatively 'beyond the pleasure principle'. The indi- vidual strives for the pleasure of gratifying the demands of his instincts and the environment compels the ego to experience displeasure at the point where it wished for pleasure, in order to avoid still worse displeasure. The technical measures to be employed for analyzing the 'defense transference' are evident from what has been said: the attitude in question must be 'isolated' from the judging ego; then it must be demonstrated that it is actively intended by the patient; finally, the anxiety which had been avoided by means of this attitude must be evoked. By carefully regulated *dosage* the analyst can protect most compulsive characters in analysis from suffering intense attacks of anxiety in the course of the treatment.

With so much emphasis on the phenomena of defense, we should not omit the consideration of 'id analysis', wrongly so called. When a patient finally admits into his preconscious representatives of instinctual impulses previously warded off and can recognize them, then we can and should call his attention to them. The fear has been expressed that what thus comes into consciousness is not the instinctual impulse but something that renders it harmless, a game, because any- thing is permitted in analysis but in real life everything remains unchanged. In my opinion this objection is sometimes

[50] Freud: *Beyond the Pleasure Principle.* London: Hogarth Press, 1922, Chap. III.

justified. When such a resistance is present, it must be interpreted. Commonly however, the 'analytic atmosphere of tolerance' brings about the contrary and imparts the courage necessary for an attempt to experience the instinctual impulses.
It is possible to make thoroughly effective discoveries of
impulses in oneself which leave no doubt concerning the reality
and affective vividness of what is experienced without having
really to live them out at the moment, but be able to subject
them *in statu nascendi* to the critical judgment of the ego.
Finally even the content of the instincts becomes 'the surface'.

Is there something corresponding to 'ego analysis' and 'id
analysis' that may be called 'superego analysis'? To analyze
the superego is to trace back to their historical foundations
defensive attitudes undertaken at the behest of the superego—
and this is especially important when these attitudes are also
expressions of instinctual attitudes returning from repression,
as is the case in moral masochism. Superego analysis is partly
an analysis of emotional relationships to persons in the environment who have been incorporated into the superego, and partly
an analysis of the early history of the instincts. With some
patients this will not require any special effort on the part of
the analyst, since what has been called 'the education of the ego
to ever greater tolerance' is indeed nothing else but a gradual
alteration of the superego.

That the analyst should carry on his work of interpretation
from a position equidistant from ego, id, and superego, is a
rule suggested by Anna Freud [51] which can be paraphrased as
meaning that the analyst must see all three aspects of psychic
phenomena and in the struggle between them remain neutral.
Essentially however, he begins always to work with the ego
and only through the ego can he reach the id and the superego; in this sense he is always closer to the ego than to the
other two.

[51] Freud, Anna: *The Ego and the Mechanisms of Defense.*   London:
Hogarth Press, 1937.   p. 30.

V

Comments on the Analysis of the Transference

It would be well to give examples for most of the points discussed hitherto; but to demonstrate what has been said would require the inclusion of entire case histories which is here not possible. We must instead progress from the discussion of 'defense transference', a special case, to the general subject of transference, the most important special area in the realm of interpretation, which has so often been referred to here but not yet considered as a whole.

Disguised or not, driving towards action or relegated to mere ideas, impulses are experienced which are inappropriate to the situation in which they arise. Unsuitable reactions to environmental stimuli, they make use of present reality only to afford a substitutive discharge for otherwise repressed forces. Even when this process goes on to the point of acting out, the discharge achieved upon such a basis is never sufficient, just as catharsis alone is insufficient. What is necessary for adequate discharge is not a single discharge of tension but a permanent dissolution of the countercathexis. Only thus is guaranteed both the liberation of energy hitherto bound up in the defense conflict and the necessary condition that somatically newly produced instinctual demands will continue to find an avenue of discharge open. Acting out may be an eruption of the id although in a disguised form. (The remobilization of old anxieties upon the threat of such an eruption brings about in the transference a repetition not only of the instinct but also of the specific defense.) Such an eruption can be utilized by the resistance in an obvious manner. The patient wishes through it gratification of impulses instead of their confrontation with the ego, wishes a short-circuited substitute for the instincts warded off by means of the 'artificial transference neurosis', in order to spare himself further surmounting of resistances. But acting out too can become a resistance in a less obvious manner, in so far as the hitherto warded off but now

recognized unconscious impulses are experienced not in their
correct context but isolated from their true objects, and in as
much as the defensive fixations are strengthened by this
isolation instead of being dissolved.

Everyone's life is full of 'transferences'. In comparison with
analytic transference two distinctions present themselves.
(1) All actions of human beings are a mixture of reactions
suited to various reality situations, and of transference. The
more impulses one must banish into the unconscious by countercathexis and which thus are likely to be expressed as 'derivatives', the greater will be the 'transference component' of an
individual's acts. *(2)* When the realities to which an individual
reacts have a relatively constant, uniform character, the transference components become still clearer; likewise the *demon-
strability* of the transference nature of these components is then
greater. People in an individual's environment react to the
individual's actions, call forth new reactions, and thus confuse
the picture. The analyst, on the contrary, is a 'mirror'; he acts
to influence the feelings of the patient as little as possible, and
the transference character of these feelings must therefore
become so much the clearer. Therefore the analyst must regard
everything that occurs in the treatment, whatever it may be,
exclusively as material, and he may not react to the analysand's
emotional storms with emotion in return; hence the require-
ment that the analyst himself have been analyzed.

The statement that the analyst is only a 'mirror' has been
misunderstood. It has been correctly emphasized that the personality of the analyst influences the transference.[52] Different
analysts act differently and these differences influence the
behavior of patients. Thus, as is well known, the sex of the
analyst plays a rôle decisive for the character of the transference
reactions of many patients. It is remarkable that with other
patients the sex of the analyst appears to be quite a matter of
indifference. They can react with both father and mother
transferences to analysts of both sexes in quite the same way.
One is again and again astonished by the *relative* insignificance

[52] Bibring-Lehner, Grete: *A Contribution to the Subject of Transference
Resistance.* Int. J. Psa., XVII, 1936. pp. 181–189.

of the actual occurrences during analysis that serve as occasions for transference reactions.

In what is called 'handling of the transference', 'not joining in the game' is the principal task. Only thus is it possible subsequently to make interpretations. The interpreting of transference reactions, it seems to me, presents no special problem; everything that has been said about interpretation in general, holds true for analysis of the transference: the surface first of all, the defense before the instinct—the interpretation must be timely, not too deep and not too superficial; particularly necessary, preceding the interpretation, is 'isolation' from the critical ego. This isolation corresponds to a cleavage of the ego into an experiencing and a judging portion, which with the aid of an identification with the analyst teaches the patient to differentiate present and past.[53] A successful interpretation of the transference must liberate new warded off derivatives and deeper layers, and as in all interpretation, proves to be a further step in fitting together the separate parts in the mosaic of the entire case. These are the valid criteria for the correctness of an interpretation.

Little is written about the very important practical subject of *countertransference*. The analyst like the patient can strive for direct satisfactions from the analytic relationship as well as make use of the patient for some piece of 'acting out' determined by the analyst's past. Experience shows that the libidinal strivings of the analyst are much less dangerous than his narcissistic needs and defenses against anxieties. Little is said about this subject probably because nothing can act as a protection against such misuse of analysis except the effectiveness of the analyst's own analysis and his honesty with himself. If the analyst knows what is going on within himself, though he will not therefore be free from sympathies and antipathies for example, he will control them. Whether the analyst should be angered by resistances of his patients or should welcome them

[53] Sterba, Richard: *Zur Dynamik der Bewältigung des Übertragungswiderstandes.* Int. Ztschr. Psa., XV, 1929. [Eng. trans. The Psa. Quarterly, IX, No 3, 1940. Ed.]

(because they offer an opportunity for the analysis of defenses) seems to me a ridiculous question. Whoever is blocked in any piece of work to which he is devoted, becomes annoyed; whoever foresees a new advance in knowledge is always glad. The point is that we should allow neither vexation nor pleasure to impede us in the patient observation and historical understanding of the resistances. A clear picture of the variety of misuses of analysis by the analyst is obtained through training analyses and supervised work.

There is another danger connected with countertransference: fear of the countertransference may lead an analyst to the suppression of all human freedom in his own reactions to patients. One analyst wished to forbid analysts to smoke in order that they might be *exclusively* a 'mirror'. I have often been surprised at the frequency with which I hear from patients who had previously been in analysis with another analyst, that they were astonished at my 'freedom' and 'naturalness' in the analysis. They had believed that an analyst is a special creation and is not permitted to be human! Just the opposite impression should prevail. The patient should always be able to rely upon the 'humanness' of the analyst. The analyst is no more to be permitted to isolate analysis from life than is a patient who misuses lying on an analytic couch for that same purpose of isolation.

The question as to whether the analyst should smoke during his work is perhaps justified from another viewpoint. Incidental activities of an autoerotic nature, playing and the like, may under certain circumstances facilitate free floating attention; under other circumstances they may be disturbing. This depends upon whether such activities afford a channel for the release of interfering libidinal impulses which, thus diverted, can no longer do any harm, or whether they augment the libidinal tension of the analyst and thus divert his attention from the patient. Whether the one or the other is the case depends upon the libido economy of the analyst. The question is identical with the problem: under what circumstances is satisfaction through fantasy a *substitute* for real satisfaction (thus causing the instinctual desire to disappear); and under what circumstances does fantasied satisfaction merely heighten instinctual tension so that subsequently the individual requires real satisfactions with a still stronger craving. In general, we may conclude, the continual devotion of attention to the patient, imposes upon the analyst so great a damming up of libido that a mild discharge like smoking is more likely than not to be beneficial. The opposite however can be the case.

VI

Working Through and Some Special Technical Problems

Psychoanalytic therapy includes an abundance of phenomena. The aim in these discussions has been to provide a perspective at the cost of details; to direct attention not only to the trees but also to the forest. We have reviewed *interpretation* from the dynamic, economic, and structural points of view, have discussed the elaboration of derivatives, the demonstration of them, the alteration thus caused in the patient's attitude of resistance, and the ensuing appearance of less distorted derivatives which are in turn treated in the same way. There should now follow a demonstration of how all this does away with the isolation from the total personality of what was previously warded off, of how the arrested development is set in motion and infantile sexuality transformed into adult sexuality so that satisfaction of instinct, and condemnation and sublimation of instinct become possible. What the analyst contributes to all these results is always merely the interpretation of new material. Although there are infinitely many more problems about details of interpretation, nevertheless we are *essentially* through with the discussion in accordance with Freud's dictum that instruction in analytic technique may be compared with learning to play chess. The opening and concluding situations are typical and relatively easy to present in their rudiments; the complications of the intermediate moves are too diverse and can be learned only from actual cases.[54] The details in the course of an analysis that fill with vivid life the structural framework we set up at the beginning become more and more plastic, the perspective

[54] Freud: *Further Recommendations in the Technique of Psycho-Analysis.* Coll. Papers, Vol. II. London: Hogarth Press, 1933. p. 342.

more and more difficult. To be sure, there comes a certain point in the analysis of an individual, just as in the analysis of a single dream, where the material which first seemed to be dispersed in all directions and to be scattered about in an abundance of complications converges rapidly upon definite and decisive points. Essentially in all of this, the activity of the analyst remains always the same: interpretation.

The inclusion of the warded off components in the total personality comes about through a special type of interpretation called 'working through'. This can be described as follows.

We have already discussed how the interpretation of a defense is accomplished. We must first isolate the defensive attitude from the judging part of the ego. The patient gradually learns that he himself is really actively bringing about what he believed he was undergoing passively. Then he learns in order: that this activity of his has a purpose; that this purpose is to evade certain matters; that what he wishes to evade is historically determined as is also the reason why he carries out the evasion in just this way. Finally he finds out how he mistakenly draws the past into the present, not having learned to differentiate between the two. Let us assume that all this has succeeded, that the patient has changed in some ways, has become more mobile, more elastic, brings new material; what was previously a general manner of behavior now appears appropriately only in special situations, and so forth. This continues for a while; then comes the next greater resistance. This can arise from the material when the analysis strikes upon something against which the defense is still greater, or it can come from an external cause which disturbs the relative equilibrium between instinct and defense, or as is mostly the case it can come through a combination of both these factors, that is, an external circumstance that has some special significance at just this stage of the analysis. The resistance now recreates the very same state that had prevailed before our first interpretation of defense. All that was won

by painstaking labor seems to be forgotten. We have to begin
again from the beginning. Sometimes it is sufficient to remind
the patient of the previous discussions of the resistance, and
the picture changes; the resistance takes on a somehow different aspect, and we must now grasp and elaborate this new
factor. Mostly, however, such a reminder does *not* suffice.
The patient becomes again as he was formerly: continually
angry or continually compliant or emotionless or proving himself innocent or anxious or in love. One gets the impression
that everything has been in vain. Once more it is necessary
to begin 'from the defense side', 'from the surface'. To be
sure, this second discussion of the same matter goes somewhat
more easily and more quickly. But even this is no protection against a third repetition with the next new stronger
resistance. Again and again whenever the resistance appears,
the original picture is reëstablished if only for a short duration
in the later stages. From time to time we penetrate one layer
deeper, but almost always or at least very often we must begin
again from the beginning.

It is not always true that a defense that has been analyzed
reappears as a new resistance, but rather that the defensive
attitude which has been surmounted in one connection may
still be operating in another. We have previously pointed out
that an interpretation is most effective when that which has
just been described in words can be demonstrated simultaneously to the patient in his behavior at another point where he
does not expect it, at 'another level'. An appropriate formulation for this process might be: 'There too!'. This 'there
too' should often be supplemented by 'there again!'. This is
specially effective when the patient is thinking of something
quite different, is searching in a quite different direction. We
are dealing here with *variants* of the same instinctual or
defensive behavior; or sometimes not even with variants but
with the appearance of *exactly the same* instinctual or defensive
behavior in different contexts.

The process that requires demonstrating to patients the same
thing again and again at different times or in various connec-

tions, is called, following Freud, 'working through'.[55] Most interpretations have this repetitive character. What makes this repetition of interpretations necessary and how is it effective? We have discussed why there is no value in 'bombarding the patient with deep interpretations' which are not yet represented in the preconscious. But why does not an interpretation suffice given *just once* if it is dynamically and economically correct and quite properly presented?

We are accustomed to say to our patients that a psychic structure which has maintained itself for years or decades cannot be done away with all at once; and that is correct. We now wish to understand theoretically why this is so. If through an interpretation the ego were changed in its defensive behavior and no longer put up the same resistance, there would not need to be a reappearance of the same behavior which had seemed to be the result of a dynamic conflict now supposed to be altered. It is simply that the ego does *not* completely relinquish its resistant attitude because of a single demonstration. It is necessary to take quite seriously the dynamic picture of a conflict. We have given warning, for example, against drawing from the techniques of distortion in the manifest content of dreams too many conclusions concerning the final relative strengths of the forces in an instinctual conflict. The relative distribution of forces, which in a single night gives final form to a dream, can be altered in a few hours. The imponderables in a living instinctual conflict that can for a fleeting time impart a small fragment of predominance now to the instinct and now to the anxiety opposing it are too numerous. To be sure, our interpretations are by no means imponderables—at least they should not be because we make a special effort to weigh them correctly from the economic point of view; nevertheless there are present in every interpretation a number of factors analogous to those imponderables, influences of the transference or of experience which alter the momentary quantitative ratio between instinct and anxiety. An initial

[55] Freud: *Recollection, Repetition and Working Through.* Coll. Papers, II. London: Hogarth Press, 1933. pp. 375–376.

improvement from the resistant attitude can retrogress entirely or partially as a result of such momentary factors. Never for example can a *single* interpretation include *all* situations in which a certain type of castration anxiety had been aroused.

The comparison of working through with the *work of mourning* (Rado) seems to me very apt. A person who has lost a friend must in all situations which remind him of this lost friend make clear to himself anew that he has this friend no longer and that a renunciation is necessary. The conception of this friend *has representation* in many complexes of memories and wishes, and the detachment from the friend must take place separately in each complex.[56] The pathogenic situations and conflicts that continue as well to have an effect, are not factors appearing just once but are represented in various complexes of ideas. Again and again the patient must in analysis reëxperience 'there too' and 'there again'. We have stated that the task in analysis is the *confrontation of the ego* with that which was warded off. In the unconscious everything is condensed, implicit, indeed without words; in the ego things are explicit. To discover something in oneself, to put it into words, is never a process that happens suddenly. Working through is the form in which the 'confrontation with the ego' takes place. The effective factor in it is *rediscovery*.

At this point there may be interpolated a digression concerning the concept of 'anticipatory ideas'. This concept seems to be the antithesis of 'surprise'. When however something that is anticipated in general appears at a special point or in a definite connection where it was actually *not* expected, then the surprise is *augmented* by the fact that in general it was expected. Let us assume that we had correctly elaborated some material analytically but that it had been forgotten or rather was not expected at just the point at which it reappeared. In such an instance the anticipatory idea is effective. We can also purposefully make use of this effect in the

---

[56] Freud: *Mourning and Melancholia*. Coll. Papers, IV. London: Hogarth Press, 1934. pp. 152–170.

following circumstances: when in the case of a patient who tends to act things out we get the impression that sometime in a state of resistance he will wish to leave the analysis, we can then prophesy this event to him and add that he will at that later time rationalize his behavior. We shall then, we tell him, remind him of today's warning to him. If what was expected actually comes about, the patient's surprise at the fact and manner of fulfilment of the prophecy may well contribute to overcoming the impulse to leave analysis and to recognizing its resistance character. On the other hand I believe there is danger in the analyst's prophesying a definite mental content to be expected, such as the content of the œdipus complex, in order to present anticipatory ideas or as an encouragement to the patient to look for such mental contents within himself. The patient becomes familiar with these contents as mere mental games before he has any experiences to correspond to them, and the analyst has discharged all his ammunition before the time when he really needs it.

Working through is a protracted process and in this respect is the antithesis of abreaction which takes place the moment an interpretation is given. Previously abreaction was considered the most effective factor in the treatment.[57] We remember how Freud explained laughter on the basis of instinct economics.[58] Energy previously bound up in the defense struggle becomes overabundantly available and explodes in laughter. That sort of liberation of energy takes places in miniature with every correct interpretation; therefore the well-known almost witty character of successful interpretations and the frequent laughter after them. However, is what is thus achieved a true and permanent dissolution of the defense struggle? Such a liberation of energy also appears in the discharge of any derivative which affords a relatively small diminution of tension. Analysis to be sure consists of a summation of such discharges

[57] Breuer and Freud: *Studien über Hysterie* (4th Edition). Vienna: Franz Deuticke, 1922.

[58] Freud: *Wit and Its Relation to the Unconscious.* New York: Moffat, Yard and Company, 1916.

of derivatives; but it is a *summation* that is required and indeed a gradual one because the ego must be made capable of assimilating this summation. Not only must previously bound energies become free in a single act, but somatically newly produced instinctual tension must permanently be able to find discharge. Therefore while all adherents of 'neo-catharsis' do not greatly value working through, all those who lay emphasis on working through see in the emotional reactions of a patient a *source of material* sometimes of significance but at other times functioning only in the service of resistance. They regard abreaction as an opportunity to demonstrate that 'that also happens' and as an introduction to the ensuing therapeutically effective *working through* of what comes to light therein; but they do not regard abreaction as therapy in itself. This conception makes clear what we must think of so called 'acting out' from the therapeutic point of view. In individuals who do not indulge in it generally, acting out is a welcome sign that in the analysis something has happened which we can and must utilize in finding out the unconscious processes behind it. On the other hand, with individuals who indulge in it frequently, acting out is resistance, that is, a means of distorting the true connections and evading a confrontation with the ego.

Especially to be emphasized at this point is that working through is working *upon* the ego; it is a process of 'confronting' the ego, and the abolition of the isolation of warded off instinct components from the total personality.

But this leads us to an apparent contradiction. For simplification we considered resistance as equivalent to the 'resistance of repression'; but we stated that there is an additional form of resistance according to Freud, a 'resistance of the id'.[59] This resistance is due to inertia in the psychic life of human beings. That which has once become canalized, remains. People gradually become less elastic, more rigid, can no longer acquire in relation to objects and life situations attitudes which are

[59] Freud: *The Problem of Anxiety.* New York: The Psa. Quarterly Press and W. W. Norton & Co., Inc., 1936. pp. 137–139

different from the habitual ones. The degree of this inertia is constitutionally variable. We know that we have no way of influencing the id directly and often indeed we are really helpless against such resistance of the id. (We may mention in this connection that analysis is contraindicated in advanced age.) Freud states however that working through is a weapon in the battle against this form of resistance.[60] But how can that be when we seem to have demonstrated that working through operates particularly upon the ego? This is apparently a contradiction.

It is indeed true that working through influences the resistance of the id; but it does this only *indirectly*. When a person is afraid but experiences a situation in which what was feared occurs without any harm resulting, he will not immediately trust the outcome of his new experience; however the second time he will have a little less fear, the third time still less. Or a person who has renounced something experiences a temptation. He will resist it once, a second time less, a third time still less. It is the *repetition* that seduces him and persuades him finally that in the future things no longer need to be the way they had always been previously; a new state of affairs can come about which need not be frightening. These are the ways in which working through operates. It attacks directly only the ego whose defensive attitude is altered. We cannot do more and can do nothing else.

It has been asked why we cannot, in order to shorten analyses, make use of advances in the special theory of neuroses which enable us to recognize at once from the diagnosis the typical instinctual conflict from which the patient is suffering. The desire is to make the analyst's knowledge immediately utilizable in practice by means of early interpretation of the determining conflicts. But that is impossible. First, what is necessary is the recognition not of 'the œdipus complex' but of the unique origin and form of a particular œdipus complex. In the second place, the factors discussed above that make working

60 *Ibid.*

through necessary, prohibit such a quick success. The ego is able only gradually to master impulses previously warded off through looking at them repeatedly always in new variant forms. Experience proves that longer analyses are the better ones. To be sure it is not the length alone that accounts for this. An analyst's 'floating along' in a patient's material for years only magnifies more and more a chaotic situation. Long systematic analytic work always gives better results than a short period of analysis.

We shall now reconsider the question of superego resistance. Is our assertion correct that this resistance proceeds only from the ego which strives to avoid penalties from the superego? Let us consider cases in which the superego resistance dominates the picture, for example moral masochism with negative therapeutic reaction. The superego itself appears like a part of the id; its impulses give exactly the same impression as in other cases do the impulses belonging to a repressed instinct. These impulses from the superego should be treated in analysis exactly like any other repressed impulses. As we know, repressed impulses can find in acting out a substitute expression unrecognized by the ego. The part played by the defensive forces in acting out that makes it a resistance is the disruption of the original connections.

Therefore when a person himself defeats every possibility for success in life, or blocks every move towards success in analysis, the process may be considered an acting out proceeding from a repressed impulse of the superego. Theoretically therefore the task is the same as in the case of any acting out of an instinctual impulse: we must show the patient that he has such an impulse, after the preceding demonstration that he is warding off some impulse. Then we must make clear to him again *why* he has such an impulse from the *defense side*. The difficulty in dealing with the negative therapeutic reaction is essentially the same as in the case of the sexualization of talking. In both cases our therapeutic instrument is usurped by the instinctual conflict. The question presented by superego resistance is why the demands of the superego have such an instinct-like character. Since superego function originated from instinctual impulses, it is a kind of fixation or regression.[61] The explanation for it is given by analysis of the history of the libidinal and aggressive relations to the object that were introjected into the superego. A negative therapeutic reaction need not always have a very complicated structure. It becomes especially intelligible when the concept either of health or of getting well is unconsciously connected with certain fantasies which are feared. In that case, in comparison with what is feared, the neurotic sufferings still remain the lesser evil and the *status quo* remains better than what might come about.

However a need for punishment is not always hidden in every state of resistance that objectively brings the patient displeasure. In most cases the reverse, a fear of punishment, motivates the ego in its resistant behavior which then brings with it displeasure unwanted by the ego, or it may be an active anticipation of punishment or the affirmation of a lesser evil in order to avoid a greater one; moreover the need for punishment when it appears, can be shown to be subordinate to a need for absolution: every attempt has to be made to free oneself of a pressure from the superego. If displeasure is temporarily necessary, it is also accepted as part of the bargain; if the process succeeds without displeasure, so much the better. Punishment and forgiveness (or forgiveness through punishment) are archaic types of relationship to an object which in the transference can easily be felt by patients in situations in which they have no place; therefore special precaution must be taken. The analyst should always create an analytic atmosphere of tolerance: 'You will not be punished here so give your "derivatives" free rein'. He should never explicitly offer

[61] 'Conscience and morality arose through overcoming, desexualizing, the œdipus-complex; in moral masochism morality becomes sexualized afresh, the œdipus-complex is reactivated, a regression from morality back to the œdipus-complex is under way.' Freud: *The Economic Problem in Masochism.* Coll. Papers, II. London: Hogarth Press, 1933. p. 266.

forgiveness (not to mention punishment) because that would mean complicity in the patient's transference reactions. He must be aware that even when he says nothing he may be considered as a forgiver or a punisher. It is a misuse of analysis by the patient, a transference reaction that brings retribution when it is not recognized by the analyst.

At this point it is appropriate to examine another problem: the question of the so called 'active' or 'passive' behavior of the analyst. We have just described the possibility that the analyst, in the unconscious of the patient, can become a punisher, a repeater of childhood castration threats, or a magician waving away the threats. This possibility seems to me to be the danger in Ferenczi's proposal of a so called active technique.[62]

But first a preliminary question: is 'active technique' the correct term for commands and prohibitions from the analyst? In making interpretations (for example interpretations of ways of behaving about which the patient himself does not speak) the analyst can and must be very active, and even when he is passive he can command or forbid. If to be active means to talk and under certain circumstances to propose subjects for association and discussion, then just as often as there is a too active behavior of the analyst, there certainly is a too passive behavior as well; and through such passivity the analyst can miss some of the interpretations which are correct from the economic point of view. Frequently the analyst has to take very active steps if he wishes to give economically correct interpretations. In periods relatively free of resistance we can confidently leave the guidance of the analysis to the patient; in times of resistance, activity on the part of the analyst is necessary. What shall we say, however, about the rule which is sometimes heard that we should 'leave the patient alone when he is in a state of resistance'? My opinion is that this rule as a generalization is simply incorrect. To be sure there are at times situations in which leaving the patient alone in this fashion demonstrates

[62] Ferenczi, Sandor: *Further Contributions to the Theory and Technique of Psycho-Analysis.* London: Hogarth Press, 1926. pp. 68–77, 198–230, 235–237.

his resistance better than would talking to him; in such cases leaving him to his own devices is what we must do in order to isolate his attitude and make it assailable. But otherwise we must work with him actively just at the time when he is in resistance.

There is a caricature of the analyst's passivity that consists in his not paying attention to the point of falling asleep. Continually analyzing in a state of free floating attention many hours daily, year after year, in all states of mind, such a thing may happen to anyone. It may be excusable but there can nevertheless be no doubt that it is a serious *mistake*. One should never allow oneself such a mistake although it would be less disastrous in a well-running, relatively resistance-free analysis where the patient can practically work by himself anyway. The misfortune is that in practice this type of mistake occurs most readily under the opposite conditions where a patient is himself sleepy and empty of affect and wishes to seduce the analyst into carelessness. Least of all should it happen in such cases, and as an excuse for its occurrence under such conditions the rule of 'leaving the patient alone in states of resistance' must not be misused.

Let us consider Ferenczi's active technique in its more limited meaning. The ideal analytic technique consists in the analyst's doing nothing other than interpreting, and·the ideal handling of the transference too, consists in not letting oneself be seduced into anything else. This ideal technique can often be reinforced by the analyst's emphasizing the fact that he is reacting to the patient quite otherwise than the patient's parents formerly reacted and differently from the way his customary environment generally reacts. Even though he influence the transference through interpretations and not by any other means, nevertheless the analyst's attitudes are continually taking part in the process. It will depend upon the situation whether he reveal more or less friendliness in his tone of voice, in the content of his remarks, or to what extent he alternate between a more friendly and a less friendly attitude. Such attitudes must under no condition be merely

shammed.   Commands and prohibitions can certainly pro-
mote the flow of feeling in certain advanced analytic situations,
but they always involve dangers of joining in the acting out
of the patient.   We have discussed this matter at length in
connection with the question of recommending asceticism.
Recommendations or prohibitions from the analyst are useful
as aids in analysis if the analyst knows precisely when he should
apply them and why, and the danger of blurring the transference picture should not be allowed to overshadow the advantages of such procedures.   What has been done and the
patient's reaction to it must subsequently be interpreted and
worked through as soon as possible after the occurrence.[63]

Throughout the psychoanalytic process the instinct components previously warded off gradually find their connections with the ego.   They catch up with the development
through which the ego had passed without them; and this new
thrust of instinct development begins at the point where
because of anxiety the defense process had set in at the earlier
time.   In place of reaction formations (in which a countercathexis prevents discharge, or at most affords a spasmodic
discharge of derivatives in acting out) more and more there
appear ways of behaving in accordance with the type of
instinctual activity or of sublimation in which an adequate
discharge takes place.   Sexual behavior changes especially.
In order for us to be able to judge the extent of his change
and of the fears that sometimes continue to oppose it, it is
often necessary to have the patient describe to us in detail his
experiences during the sexual act and during the orgasm.   But
this description should come about at its natural time, and not
through an insistence of the analyst that sometimes gives the
impression of a monomania.

In this new adaptation of the sexual behavior, the reality
situation often creates great difficulties.   The analysis is aided
by every opportunity for sexual satisfaction at a time when the
patient is becoming capable of a different and adult sexual

[63] This was also the opinion of Ferenczi.

activity. I can confirm the fact that particularly in final phases of an analysis, if opportunity for sexual satisfaction is lacking, we find that in place of the previous psychoneurosis, *actual-neurotic* symptoms appear, resulting from damming up of normal libido capable of discharge but having no outlet.[64] In this situation there are frequently conflicts between instincts and wish for recovery on the one hand and ideals of marriage or other ideals on the other hand. In my opinion there can certainly be reality considerations that are decisive. Sometimes a real suffering which by virtue of the complete cessation of the neurosis is fully experienced by the patient for the first time, or a real suffering by which others are threatened, is greater than the neurotic suffering due to unanalyzed remainders; and even a partial success is meritorious if we are aware of its limits and uncertainty. On the other hand, in those cases in which considerations for example of the real interests of other people are not decisive, but where it is a question merely of 'ideals', I believe that if we do not break off the analysis too soon and if we consistently show the patient his intrapsychic reality, he will recognize that clinging to inappropriate ideals and moralities has a resistance function. He will then begin to think as well about the significance of the circumstance under which such inappropriate ideals were learned. It has been said that religious people in analysis remain uninfluenced in their religious philosophies since analysis itself is supposed to be philosophically neutral. I consider this not to be correct. Repeatedly I have seen that with the analysis of the sexual anxieties and with maturing of the personality, the attachment to religion has ended.

When it is said that analysis should in the end make it possible for the patient to adapt to reality, this has been interpreted to mean that analysts believe patients who are cured should regard as unchangeable those circumstances of life to which they are now exposed and should adapt themselves to them. Nowhere in Freud's writings can anything of the sort

[64] Reich, Wilhelm: *Charakteranalyse*. Vienna, 1933 (published by the author).

be found. I fear however that among analysts this opinion may occasionally be expressed. Such an interpretation is *wrong*. Adaptation to reality means nothing else than the ability to judge *rationally* both reality and the probable results of one's own actions. But to judge the probable results of one's actions and to regulate one's actions accordingly, does not mean to accept all given circumstances. There exists as well the so called *alloplasticity*, the possibility of altering reality in conformity with one's wishes.

An objection has been raised to the view of the preponderant therapeutic significance of a well regulated sexual economy. It has been said that the successes of child analysis are not explainable according to such a conception. In my opinion there actually is a difference in this respect between the analysis of adults and child analysis. Whereas the satisfaction of instincts which had previously been fended off represents the essential therapeutic factor in the analysis of adults, we are forced in child analysis to forbid direct satisfaction to a large portion of the instincts that are set free. I believe that Edith Jacobssohn is right in her statement that the results of child analysis are therefore a degree more uncertain than those of the analysis of adults.[65] That practical results of child analysis are nevertheless possible is apparently due to the circumstance that masturbation, tolerated sexual games and aim inhibited relationships to objects represent substitutes. Besides this we must agree that the question of an infantile orgasm has not yet been settled; that is, the question as to how the sexual economy before puberty is physiologically regulated. As is well known, before the development of the primacy of the genital and with it a specifically adapted apparatus for satisfaction, excitement and satisfaction are not so strictly separated from each other as they are after puberty.[66] End-pleasure is

[65] Jacobssohn, Edith: *Zum Heilungsproblem in der Kinderanalyse.* Paper read at the XIIIth Internat. Psa. Congress. Reviewed by the author in Int. Ztschr. Psa., XXI, 1935, p. 331.

[66] Freud: *Three Contributions to the Theory of Sex.* New York and Washington: Nervous and Mental Disease Publ. Co., 1930. p. 69.

not so sharply separated from forepleasure. Experience however shows that excitement and satisfaction, forepleasure and
end-pleasure, are not therefore simply identical with one
another. Their boundaries are not sharp, but they comprise
different spheres nevertheless. Even before puberty there is
a relative orgasm, and satisfaction consists in a discharge which
has no single definite end point so that the satisfaction cannot
be sharply differentiated from the excitement. Since there is
a discharge, the damming up is diminished by it. Making
possible instinctual satisfaction appropriate for the child seems
to me therefore the goal of child analysis just as the aim of
analysis of adults is to make possible the instinctual satisfaction
of which adults are capable. Of course I do not wish with
these statements to minimize the significance of the primacy of
the genital or the special importance of genitality.

A further question is the one concerning the break up of the
superego which is supposed to take place in the analytic cure.
Certainly the destruction of the archaic portion of the superego, the ending of the automatically occurring repetition of
instinct prohibitions, which at one time in the past had been
considered justified, is necessary. However, the category of
'I ought to', the possibility of evaluating and the possibility of
being satisfied or dissatisfied with oneself, of having stirrings
of conscience, all these remain in every healthy person as a
matter of course. But in spite of this it seems to me correct
that unequivocally one part of the instinct-regulating functions carried out in the neurotic by the superego must be taken
over by the ego: automatic allowance or rejection of instinctual
temptations must be replaced by judgment of the real consequences of prospective instinctual actions. Reason replaces
the superego, but not entirely. There remain situations in
which differences continue to arise between ego and superego,
and they are the ones in which one has a feeling of guilt.
Apart from that however, the spheres of ego and superego fuse
very considerably in the healthy person.

Influencing the superego comes about gradually during
analytic treatment. This we have designated as 'the education

of the ego to a tolerance of less and less distorted derivatives'. It is clear that in this process a large rôle is played by the identification of the patient with the analyst. However we should not call it an 'introjection of the analyst by the patient' whenever an analyst convinces his patient of some truth.[67] In neuroses in which the superego front of the ego plays a greater rôle in the pathogenic conflicts, it is furthermore necessary to analyze the *origins* of the superego.

It is often said that the ego must be enabled to condemn the infantile sexual impulses unconsciously operative in the neurotic after repression of them has been abolished. Since this might be misunderstood, I should like explicitly to emphasize that as a rule such a condemnation is no separate act which the individual must voluntarily carry out. In occasional cases it happens that the abolition of a repression leads at first to experiencing a certain perverse impulse and the indulgence in perverse sexual activities. Such activities are temporary and are historically conditioned; and for this temporary perverse phase to be brought to an end, further analysis of the anxieties which oppose normal sexuality is necessary. Apart from such cases, a good analysis is characterized precisely by the fact that the infantile sexual impulses in some way become—simultaneously with their attaining consciousness—*empty of content*. They are experienced as impulses actually present but experienced otherwise than they were in childhood, with a sort of astonishment of the ego as if to ask: 'What for?' or 'What could I do with that?'. The newly released infantile impulses no longer suit the ego. After removing defenses the greater part of the libido has been transformed into genital primacy and the fact that it has thus become capable of discharge makes intelligible the attitude of the ego towards the remaining infantile impulses. The capacity to sublimate the pregenital libido that remains must be greater when the major portion of the libido is genitally discharged, than it is when such genital discharge not being possible, the total sexuality requires satisfaction in an unaltered

[67] *Cf.* Strachey, James: *Symposium, III.* Int. J. Psa., XVIII, 1937, pp. 139–45.

pregenital form. Indeed there can be no doubt that when the so called condemnation becomes such a matter of course, the chief factor in the process is the relative increase of genitality and decrease of pregenitality.

One often hears it said that for the completion of an analysis a 'dissolution of the transference' is necessary. Actually the dissolution of the transference begins with the first transference interpretation, as a rule soon after the beginning of the treatment. Every correct transference interpretation leads back to its true connections a portion of the libido hitherto invested in transference, and thus dissolves transference. As we have said before, there is one form of transference we preserve as long as possible because it represents a good aid for us in our work, and that is the paradoxically so called rational transference. It too must at some time become a resistance. At that point our task becomes the dissolution of the transference in its more limited sense. The patient must learn to renounce guidance and to settle his conflicts by himself. If this is accomplished by gradually decreasing the weekly number of the patient's analytic sessions, there is no essential objection to be made to such a procedure. Such a device can never replace the analytic work by means of which the patient should become not outwardly but inwardly independent of his analyst. If this analytic work is skilfully carried out, then I do not know why such an external 'gradual weaning' should be necessary. A more emphatic and essential objection is to be made when Alexander considers such a diminution of the weekly number of analytic sessions to be indicated in the midst of an analysis in order to combat a too great dependence of the patient upon the analyst.[68] In my opinion, the use of such a method would be like a surgeon stopping his operation because during it there is more bleeding than he had expected.

A few more words are now in order concerning some frequent abnormal types of analytic reactions. We saw that it is one of the principal tasks of the analyst to prevent by correct technique the divergence of the patient's analytic work towards

[68] Alexander, Franz: Review of Kubie: *Practical Aspects of Psychoanalysis.* The Psa. Quarterly, V, 1936, p. 287.

the Scylla of too much talking or towards the Charybdis of too much feeling. But what should the analyst do when a patient on coming to analysis is already the prey of either Scylla or Charybdis?

Most frequent victims of the Charybdis of feeling are the patients who begin with a transference storm of emotion before the analyst can know what this storm signifies. These are neurotic characters who act things out. The analyst can do with them nothing other than look for a reasonable residual ego and come to an understanding with that portion of the patient's personality. He must try to show that the patient is actively carrying out some special activity that serves him a definite pur- pose, isolate his behavior from the residual ego, and continue this for as long as it is necessary, until the significance of the action becomes clear and analyzable. Sometimes we succeed thus in learning why the analysis had to begin in this manner, why the ego had to respond in the same way in the past to the first symptoms, the infantile anxieties. These patients are 'traumatophilic' persons whose characters have the structure of a traumatic neurosis and who strive all their lives to evade the repetition of a severely painful childhood impression but simultaneously seek to experience it again and again in order finally to be able to master it by continual repetition.

Most frequent victims of the Scylla of mere talking are per- sons who are empty of affect or cold in their feelings; who have learned to escape disagreeable experiences by isolation of affect and ideational content. When affects are completely lacking the defensive function of this lack is relatively easy to demon- strate. One need then only guard against the mistake of analyzing contents which to the patient would be interesting conversation, while no work at all would be done at points decisive from the economic viewpoint. More difficult are patients with pseudo-affects, persons who are always stirred up or always have to be acting some part. We should recall what has been said about 'threefold stratification' and should pay particular attention to the latent negative transference that can be hidden behind a positive front.

Above all the transference should be interpreted when it has become a resistance.[69] However, it must be noted that this is not always easy because the first resistances are not always clearly recognizable as such. We consider a patient as relatively free of resistance when he shows a rational attitude toward analysis and seems ready to coöperate. But why should a person really have confidence right from the start in a strange individual and in a strange and implausible procedure? A too great readiness to behave rationally is therefore also suspicious. A person should have a normal distrust and where it is completely lacking, the suspicion is justified that it is repressed. Analyzing the negative transference does not always mean asking an angry patient, 'Why are you angry with me?' but often rather inquiring, 'Why do you not dare to show that you have feelings of anger against me?'. There is a type of patient in whom the defense against even his slightest unfriendly impulse is so essential a part of his character resistance that a close attention to his associations and dreams, together with the avoidance of interpretations of content provided by him, will after long analytical effort reveal as a repressed impulse, for example, indignation over the fact that he once had to wait somewhat longer than usual in the waiting room!

On the other hand, not everything is transference that is experienced by a patient in the form of affects and impulses during the course of an analytic treatment. If the analysis appears to make no progress, the patient has in my opinion the right to be angry, and his anger need not be a transference from childhood—or rather we will not succeed in demonstrating the transference component in it; besides, there is also a life outside of the transference which continues to go on after an individual enters analytic treatment. A certain patient may have been right when he responded to a transference interpretation by saying: 'Doctor, you are surely conceited; you make everything refer to yourself!' At times we have a choice as to whether a conflict can be better analyzed on the basis of the transference to the analyst or on the basis of the behavior

[69] Freud: *Further Recommendations in the Technique of Psycho-Analysis.* Coll. Papers, II. London: Hogarth Press, 1933. p. 360.

of the patient outside analysis. The concentration of the whole
analysis in transference analysis if possible naturally has definite advantages, above all in the fact that we can observe the
origin and course of all the conflicts. There are situations in
which a correct analysis of behavior outside of the analysis
prepares the ground for or supplements such transference
analysis very well; there are also situations (for example certain
negative transferences) which if left to our choice, we prefer
to analyze on the basis of material of the 'life outside'. We
must never forget the existence of this life outside; we must
always draw it into the treatment. Otherwise there is the
danger that the patient will escape from analysis into his outside life. This is a serious danger only when the patient does
not discuss his life situation in analysis, so that the analyst
knows nothing about it. The analyst should be aware of such
an omission.

Too great warning cannot be given against isolation of
analysis from real life. The patient who misuses lying on the
couch, or who goes to the toilet before every analytic session,
contributes no more to such isolation than does the analyst by
means of faulty selection of material to discuss, by too ceremonial behavior, or by a too limited ability for seeing and
proving his points using the trifles of everyday life, and above
all by failing always to start analyzing from the surface.

A commonplace example of neglect of the significance of the
surface that made an impression on me occurred in Oslo where
an opponent of psychoanalysis once gave a lecture in which he
told of an acquaintance who was being analyzed and who,
though fifty years of age, wished still to learn ice skating. This
man practiced skating on lonely mountain lakes surrounded
by steep walls of rock. His analyst tried to convince him that
he made this choice of place out of a longing for his mother's
womb. In actuality, said the lecturer, this fifty-year-old gentle-
man wanted merely to escape spectators in less lonely places
who would have laughted at his attempts to learn skating. This
critic is absolutely right. If the behavior of the patient in
question really had the significance of a longing for his
mother's womb, such a meaning should have become accessible

to analysis through previous discussion of the attitude of shame in a more superficial layer which was overlooked by the analyst. In the analysis of men who go to prostitutes, one hears emphasized the mother significance of the prostitute or the homosexual nature of an interest in women who have intercourse with so many men. Such emphasis neglects an important layer. The essential thing about the prostitute for her client is the fact that he does not know her personally, that in going to her he completely isolates his sensuality from the rest of his life so that the sensuality does not count afterwards and can easily be 'undone'.

Because it is recognized that resistances often spring from the patient's intellect so that things are not experienced but merely thought of as possible, analysts are often misled into the opposite extreme of a depreciation of the rôle of the intellect in analysis. We can and we should make use of the patient's ability to reason at many points.

Let us summarize the points of view presented in this section of our discussion. All interpretations, and particularly the most important special case of interpretation, transference interpretation, must be made *repeatedly* at every new resistance barrier: in other words, *working through* is necessary. What is attained thereby is the union with the ego of what was previously warded off by it. The advantage of this union is that the previously excluded instinctual tendencies catch up in a development which had previously been arrested, and are given the possibility of discharge whereas previously they were dammed up. The energies that were dammed up *really* become free.

I hope I have succeeded in making intelligible what appears to me desirable in a more systematic technique. This is not to say that we should analyze with understanding alone and not with intuition, but that we should have no aversion to reflecting upon our procedures so that we may always act intuitively from knowledge and understanding and with a purpose.

VII

Comments on the Literature of Psychoanalytic Technique

What we have wished to do in our discussions up to this point was not to contribute anything really new, but to annotate the technical rules set up by Freud and to show how the freudian theory of neuroses is applied in psychoanalytic therapy. We have discussed not the historical transformations of analytic technique but its principles as actually applied at present. Now that this discussion has been completed, some remarks about its historical development will certainly be of interest, as will be also the divergence of opinion among analysts upon certain points. With reference to the latter we believe that the need for lengthy polemics has been precluded by the presentation in previous chapters of conclusions arrived at not on the basis of controversy but rather by virtue of their cogency.

The psychoanalytic literature is very extensive. It is amazing how small a proportion of it is devoted to psychoanalytic technique and how much less to the theory of technique: an explanation of what the analyst does in psychoanalysis. This state of affairs is the result first of all of difficulties in presentation with which we too have had to contend in these discussions since in our wish to describe technique we had to presuppose a knowledge of the foundations of technique; it is the result, further, of external difficulties such as the consideration that patients in analysis might read the psychoanalytic literature. Nevertheless, the scarcity of papers on technique remains astonishing. To be sure, the absolute number of such papers is considerable, as shown in the appended bibliography; but this is a relatively small number compared with the total volume of psychoanalytic literature.

I do not intend to go back to beginnings and, for example, to describe the relationship of analysis to hypnosis. I shall start at the point where, long after analysis had been introduced as a special technique, the technical papers of Freud were generally known and followed by all analysts, and Freud had proposed as the subject for a prize competition the reciprocal influence between technique and theory.[70] In 1923 appeared the book of Ferenczi and Rank, *Entwicklungsziele der Psychoanalyse*.[71] At the Congress in Salzburg in 1924, a symposium on this subject [72] was held in which Rado, Alexander, and Sachs, took part. For reasons of economy of space I can devote only a few sentences to each contribution, and I must therefore select what I consider essential and characteristic. It may be that the selection is subjective and that another might have chosen differently.

We began our discussions with a description of the eternal Scylla and Charybdis of analytic technique—too much talking versus too much feeling. In the early days of psychoanalysis the topological formula to the effect that in analysis 'the unconscious is made conscious' held sway. This formula was better known than the dynamic one, as yet not understood, that analysis must 'abolish resistances'. At that time, therefore, the greater danger was the Scylla of too much talking or intellectualization: the analyst guessed at complexes, named them and depended upon that for the cure. This might succeed if there were no special resistance isolating what was talked about from the actual point of the dynamic defense conflict. If there was such a resistance, the analyst relied in vain upon a comparison with the many cables that had to be untied one by one. As long as the main secret—resistance—remained unsolved, he might understand intellectually as much as he could about childhood and development but it

[70] Int. J. Psa., III, 1922. p. 521.
[71] In English: Ferenczi and Rank: *The Development of Psychoanalysis*. New York and Washington: Nervous and Mental Disease Publ. Co, 1925
[72] Int. J. Psa., VI, 1925. pp. 1-44.

did no good. Ferenczi's and Rank's book represented a reaction against this situation. They emphasized again and again
that analysis is not an intellectual but an affective process, a
'process of libido flow' in which emotional experiences are
relived in the transference and previously hidden material
thus revived for the ego's disposal. The authors certainly
went too far to the other extreme. In their emphasis on
experiencing they became admirers of abreaction, of acting
out, and thus working through was the loser. When we
reread the book today we get the impression that in the history of psychoanalysis Scylla periods and Charybdis periods
alternated and that it must have been very difficult to pass
evenly between the opposite dangers.

The symposium in Salzburg had a somewhat different character; it set itself the same problems as we have in these discussions. It is unfortunate that Rado's contribution [73] has
remained a fragment. He advances a theory of hypnosis and
catharsis in which he explains how the therapist makès use of
certain transference tendencies of the patient to reproduce
regressively certain archaic conditions of the ego, thus making
it possible for the therapist, or rather the patient's conception
of him, to become endowed with special authority because
the functions of the superego and many functions of the ego
have been projectively assigned to him. To be sure, the
genuine superego and ego remain. The therapist is introjected
as a 'parasite upon the superego' and also, we must add, as a
'parasite upon the ego'. His special authority is then made
use of by the therapist to induce the ego, in the case of
hypnotic suggestion therapy, to strengthen its defensive activities, in the case of hypnotic catharsis therapy, to weaken the
defensive measures. This theory works well enough except in
the following circumstance: the success in this delegation of
authority and ego regression remains closely dependent upon
the condition that the libido previously bound up in the

[73] Rado, Sandor: *The Economic Principle in Psychoanalytic Technique.*
Int. J. Psa., VI, 1925. pp. 35–44.

genuine neurosis now remains bound in a transference neurosis, the hypnotic rapport, and does not become free. A paper applying these views about hypnotic catharsis to an understanding of psychoanalysis was planned by Rado but never published. It would have explained that analysis begins similarly to an hypnotic rapport but ultimately proceeds to a *dissolution* of the transference. It would have made clear also that the development of the transference takes place in analysis not through an obvious and sudden incitement to regressions but through the opportunity for spontaneous development.

Perhaps we have not stressed sufficiently that in analysis 'transference' actually has as its content not only the repetition of old relationships in general, but of those especially in which functions that later will be taken over by ego and superego are still exercised by persons in the external world. To say that 'the analyst educates the ego to a tolerance of the instincts' is equivalent to saying that 'the analyst functions as the patient's superego' and in so doing operates otherwise than the patient's superego previously did. The 'cleavage' into an observing and an experiencing part of the ego in interpretation comes about through identification of the patient with the analyst. Strachey [74] considers this the really effective principle in interpretation, affirming Rado's earlier views.

Alexander [75] was more impressed by discoveries, new at the time, about the superego. The process of eliminating the archaic and automatic defensive activity of the ego, which takes place mostly (but not always) under the pressure of an archaic and automatically operating superego, he described by pointing out that analysis must transfer the functions of the superego to the reasonable ego, making superfluous 'the repressing power' of the superego. We have expressed the opinion that there is considerable truth in what Alexander

[74] Strachey, James: *The Nature of the Therapeutic Action of Psycho-Analysis.* Int. J. Psa., XV, 1934. pp. 127–159.

[75] Alexander, Franz: *A Metapsychological Description of the Processes of Cure.* Int. J. Psa., VI, 1925. pp. 13–35.

formulated in so radical a manner. Not only over the id but also over the superego as an absolute power beyond appeal must the ego prevail in the form of reason and reasonable judgment of actual situations adapted to present reality. However, there remains even for the healthy person the possibility of estrangement between the experiencing and the valuating functions of the ego; hence also the quality of 'ought to' and feeling of guilt.

The contribution of Sachs [76] to the symposium emphasized particularly what we have called the confrontation of the ego with the warded off contents: not single abreactions but 'the complete subordination to the secondary process' of what was previously unconscious and its 'incorporation in the ego' is what is essential for psychoanalytic therapy; only that could alter the dynamics and economics of the previous types of defense. It is noteworthy that at this time, shortly after the appearance of The Ego and the Id,[77] the differentiation between the concepts 'id' and 'unconscious ego' was not yet clear. Sachs wrote: 'The resistance then is part of the id which shelters it—above all from the demands of the ego ideal which at least, in so far as identification with the analyst has taken place, strives against the resistance.' [78] Thus he designates as 'id' the unconscious portion of the ego which is really in opposition to the id; and he designates as 'ego ideal' the reasonable ego as modified through the introjection of the analyst, which really is opposed to what we mean by ego ideal (part of the unmodified superego). This mode of expression then leads Sachs to make use of concepts in his paper otherwise than we have used them in our discussions.

In 1927 the *Internationale Zeitschrift für Psychoanalyse* published papers from the Seminar for Psychoanalytic Therapy in Vienna which attempted to bring together systematically

[76] Sachs, Hanns: *Metapsychological Points of View in Technique and Theory.* Int. J. Psa., VI, 1925. pp. 5–13.

[77] Freud: *The Ego and the Id.* London: Hogarth Press, 1927. (Original, German edition: *Das Ich und das Es.* Vienna, 1923.)

[78] Sachs, Hanns: *Loc cit.* p. 8.

the results of long case discussions and thus deal more with clinical practice than had the Salzburg symposium. Most noteworthy of these was the paper of Reich, *Zur Kritik der Deutung und der Widerstandsanalyse* [79] (An Evaluation of Interpretation and of Resistance Analysis) in which the theoretical explanations coincide extensively with our views. What was new in this paper was the way it took into consideration not only the dynamic rôle of interpretation ('removing resistance') but its *economic* aspect as well. Reich's emphasis upon being systematic in interpretations is in itself correct. The sequence of interpretations is prescribed by the sequence of the layers in the unconscious, and every deviation from this sequence causes a 'chaotic situation'. But one gets the impression that this emphasis upon systematization goes somewhat too far, or is expressed unclearly because of too extensive schematization. He takes Freud's rules of technique as his point of departure and works over them without presenting any new proposals for technique as if merely to say: 'Think continually whether you are applying the correct freudian technique.' We should not, he advises, only *say* that interpretation is a dynamic and economic process, we should consistently think it through and follow it out in that way. Do not interpret what the patient is just now talking about, but interpret at the point where the economically decisive resistance lies, and especially in relation to the character. Also in this paper Reich describes for the first time how *consistency* in interpretation promotes working through.

The first of Sterba's papers on technique [80] brings to us the application of these basic principles in a special case—the latent negative transference, in connection with which the beginner easily makes mistakes. This is followed by two more

[79] Reich, Wilhelm: *Zur Kritik der Deutung und der Widerstandsanalyse.* Int. Ztschr. Psa., XIII, 1927. pp. 141–159.

[80] Sterba, Richard: *Über latente negative Übertragung.* Int. Ztschr. Psa., XIII, 1927. pp. 160–165. *Zur Bewältigung der Dynamik des Übertragungswiderstandes.* Int. Ztschr. Psa., XV, 1929. pp. 456–470. [Eng. trans. The Psa. Quarterly, IX, No. 3, 1940. Ed.] *The Fate of the Ego in Analytic Therapy.*

important, more theoretical papers, *Zur Bewältigung der Dynamik des Übertragungswiderstandes* (The Dynamics of the Dissolution of the Transference Resistance) and The Fate of the Ego in Analytic Therapy. In these it is stated (as we too have pointed out) that the effective factor in interpretation lies in the *division* of the ego into an experiencing portion and an observing portion which results from the positive transference and an identification with the analyst. This cleavage in the patient's ego is utilized by the analyst to demonstrate the discrepancy between present and past, and this demonstration then induces the ego to alter its defensive attitude. The alteration becomes permanent by virtue of the subsequent working through.

Reich subsequently pursued further [81] in many ways the principles laid down in *Zur Kritik der Deutung und der Widerstandsanalyse,* investigating and describing their application in detail. It is the merit of his important papers to have added to the meaning of the rules: 'Interpretation of resistance precedes interpretation of content', and 'Analyze always from the surface'. In order to attain the desired dynamic and economic alteration, he said, it is necessary to recognize and name not only what is fended off but also the *defending force* itself, and this 'ego analysis' must take place systematically, consistently, and in the end historically. When a patient does not follow the basic rule of free association, the analyst must not, impatient with such unsuitable behavior, try to influence him pedagogically or punish him by depriving him of treatment; he must try to understand analytically why the patient behaves thus and why he does it just in this manner. Reich made especially clear the 'frozen character resistances', and above all the fact I have tried to show in these discussions,

81 Reich, Wilhelm: *Bericht über das Seminar für psychoanalytische Therapie am psychoanalytischen Ambulatorium in Wien 1925–1926.* Int. Ztschr. Psa., XIII, 1927. pp. 241–245. *Über Charakteranalyse.* Int. Ztschr. Psa., XIV, 1928. pp. 180–196. *Der genitale und der neurotische Charakter.* Int. Ztschr. Psa., XV, 1929. pp. 435–455.

that in many cases the thawing out at just these points is the indispensable prerequisite to any subsequent progress in analytic treatment, even when at these same points relatively fluid living conflicts between instinct and defense are concurrently observable.

With Reich's *Charakteranalyse,*[82] which brings all these conclusions together and supplements them with some new ones, we must thoroughly agree in its *essentials.* However, the objection must be made that the book gives way so extensively to some personal characteristics of its author, especially to his penchant for schematic simplification, that the work as a whole suffers. We wish therefore to qualify our essential agreement by two minor theoretical objections and by some others that are directed not against Reich's principles but against the way he applies them.[83] The two criticisms of theory refer to: *(1)* the insufficient consideration of 'faulting' and of 'spontaneous chaotic situations'; *(2)* the neglect of 'the collection of material'. Objections to the way his principles are applied are: *(1)* 'Shattering of the patient's defensive armor' is sometimes accomplished too aggressively with Reich and should be regulated by better dosage. *(2)* When a patient's aggression is mobilized by an aggressive act of the analyst, this aggression is not properly speaking a 'negative transference'; or rather, to the extent that it still is one, it loses its ability to be demonstrated as such. *(3)* Reich's preference for 'crises', 'eruptions' and theatrical emotions makes one suspicious of a 'traumatophilia' that has its roots in a love of magic. *(4)* The 'shattering of the defensive armor' is masochistically enjoyed by many patients, and specific transferences can hide behind such enjoyment and escape discovery.

In the time that has elapsed since the publication of this book, Reich has undergone an unsatisfactory development

---

[82] Reich, Wilhelm: *Charakteranalyse.* Vienna, 1933 (published by the author).

[83] *Cf.* Fenichel, Otto: *Zur Theorie der psychoanalytischen Technik.* Int. Ztschr. Psa., XXI, 1935. pp. 78–95.

which has led him entirely away from psychoanalysis. His new therapeutic efforts [84] can be criticized directly from the correct 'Reichian principles' which they contradict; their chief dangers are the falsifications of the transference and the tendency to 'traumatophilia'.

One of the stimuli to the development of so called 'analytic ego psychology' [85] was insight into the fact that *resistance* analysis is the real therapeutic agent and that pursuing the aim of analyzing resistance has as a prerequisite the thorough analytic investigation particularly of chronic attitudes of resistance anchored in an individual's character. Here again the volume of the literature concerning the newly gained psychological insight is incomparably greater than the number of papers which seek to utilize this insight to contribute to an improvement of psychoanalytic technique. For example there is a paper by Nina Searl [86] in which she strives to clarify what it means to *analyze* a resistance in contradistinction to 'refuting' a resistance. On the other hand a paper by Kaiser,[87] which I have criticized in detail elsewhere,[88] likewise calls for consistent interpretation of resistances, but for him 'interpreting a resistance' means *not* confirming its presence, finding out its purpose and immediate cause and coördinating its form with those past experiences of the patient out of which it originates, but rather logically refuting the so called 'resistant thoughts' or demonstrating their contradictions. It is remark-

[84] Reich, Wilhelm: *Psychischer Kontakt und Vegetative Strömung.* Copenhagen: Sexpol Verlag, 1935. *Orgasmus reflex, Muskelhaltung, und Körperausdruck.* Copenhagen: Sexpol Verlag, 1937.

[85] Another stimulus to development of analytic ego psychology was the circumstance that in place of the most frequent earlier forms of neurosis in which a relatively unified ego seemed to be disturbed by 'symptoms', there appeared more and more other forms of neurosis in which the ego itself seemed drawn into the pathological process.

[86] Searl, Nina: *Some Queries on Principles of Technique.* Int. J. Psa., XVII, 1936. pp. 471–493.

[87] Kaiser, Helmuth: *Probleme der Technik.* Int. Ztschr. Psa., XX, 1934. pp. 490–522.

[88] Fenichel, Otto: *Zur Theorie der psychoanalytischen Technik.* Int. Ztschr. Psa., XXI, 1935. pp. 78–95.

able that so exaggerated a rationalism is compatible with anti-rationalism upon a different point. Kaiser, an admirer of acting out, considers a 'true eruption of instinct' the sole therapeutic principle. He gives to 'resistance analysis' the further significance that the unconscious itself is no longer to be made an object of analysis at all.

Nunberg to whom we are indebted for his paper about the 'wish for recovery',[89] included in his book, *Allgemeine Neurosenlehre*, a chapter on the 'theoretical foundations of therapy'.[90] He lays great stress upon two factors as being therapeutically effective: *(1)* the 'synthetic function of the ego', which shows itself therapeutically in the tendency of the ego to assimilate immediately such contents as are newly made accessible to it and to arrange them in a purposeful coherence; *(2)* 'abreaction', or the explosive release in the act of becoming conscious, of the energy previously bound up in the conflict of repression. In previous sections of these discussions we have expressed our opinion about the rôle of abreaction.

The English school of psychoanalysis has contributed two series of lectures on technique, one by Glover[91] and one by Sharpe,[92] which show the influence of the divergent views of these analysts about the theory of neuroses, but which are very fruitful. Both present more the practice than the theory of technique. Both fail to teach principles concretely and elastically applicable to actual situations, but each gives examples of applications which afford glimpses into the subjective nature of their own work. In this they emphasize that what has been taught is example and not model, and that the correct technique is an 'art' which obtains

[89] Nunberg, Hermann: *The Will to Recovery.* Int. J. Psa., VII, 1926. pp. 64–78.

[90] Nunberg, Hermann: *Allgemeine Neurosenlehre auf psychoanalytischer Grundlage.* Berne and Berlin: Verlag Hans Huber, 1932. pp. 293–312.

[91] Glover, Edward: *Lectures on Technique in Psycho-Analysis.* Int. J. Psa., VIII, 1927. pp. 311–338 and 486–520. IX, 1928. pp. 7–46 and 181–218.

[92] Sharpe, Ella Freeman: *The Technique of Psycho-Analysis.* Int. J. Psa., XI, 1930. pp. 251–277 and 361–386. XII, 1931. pp. 24–60.

increased probability of success not through more abundant knowledge, but through the deeper analysis of the analyst himself. Sharpe's emphasis on defense analysis, particularly character analysis, coincides with our views.

A more theoretical contribution from the English school is represented by the paper of Strachey.[93] Of all the processes taking place in analysis, he lays greatest stress upon the substitution of the analyst for the patient's superego. The analyst functioning as superego uses his power to abolish that portion of the patient's own superego that requires pathogenic defense. In his investigation of the mechanisms with whose help the analyst becomes the patient's superego, Strachey relies upon the views of Melanie Klein.[94] 'The neurotic vicious circle', Strachey states, is interrupted by the analyst's offering himself to the patient as an object to be introjected. In so far as he is a 'good' object, he interferes in the circle and prevents further 'projection' of archaic and 'evil' introjected objects. The phenomenon we call 'transference upon the analyst' Strachey describes by stating that the patient projects archaic imagos, that is archaic introjected objects, upon the analyst. The patient becomes convinced however of the analyst's tolerant attitude, introjects then the 'good' interpreting analyst, and thereby neutralizes the intrapsychic archaic introjected objects that were active within him. With this as a basis Strachey analyzes interpretation, pointing out that an effective interpretation must be a 'transference interpretation', or in other words must be a matter of the *real present* at the moment in which it is offered. With this stipulation taken into account, he believes, we need not hesitate to offer 'deep' interpretations early in the analysis.

A book written by Helene Deutsch, Psycho-Analysis of the Neuroses (London: Hogarth Press, 1932), describes primarily the treatment of specific types of neuroses and contains many

[93] Strachey, James: *The Nature of the Therapeutic Action of Psycho-Analysis.* Int. J. Psa., XV, 1934. pp. 127–159.

[94] Klein, Melanie: *The Psycho-Analysis of Children.* London: Hogarth Press, 1932.

important and stimulating observations about the essentials of psychoanalytic technique in general.

An antithesis to all these attempts to *make use of our knowledge* for the development of technique is found in some works of Theodor Reik on technique. He warns that too much knowledge can be *harmful* to the analyst because it might lead him to misapplication of this knowledge and to a hampering of his intuition. In his first work on this subject, New Ways of Psychoanalytic Technique,[95] Reik went to extremes. He was constantly fearing harm from too much reflective thinking. He starts from the recognition (published in earlier papers) [96] that the realization of unconscious contents, following the elimination of repressions, always takes place with a remarkable feeling of surprise which alone, according to Reik, is dynamically and economically effective.[97] Therefore both the analyst and the patient should always be prepared for surprises. The analyst should give free play to his unconscious without any preconceived theoretical opinions, should discover everything anew in each patient. Reik apparently imagined the 'systematic techniques' against which he inveighed to be blueprints valid for all cases and to be learned by rote. In his latest book, Surprise and the Psycho-Analyst,[98] Reik has modified this standpoint in a gratifying way. In spite of polemics in favor of intuition and against too much intellect and theory in the practising analyst, this splendid book contains the best scientific theory of the mode of action of intuition.

A more recent paper on the theory of technique is one by Alexander,[99] The Problem of Psychoanalytic Technique.

[95] Reik, Theodor: *New Ways of Psychoanalytic Technique.* Int. J. Psa., XIV, 1933. pp. 321–339.

[96] Reik, Theodor: *Der Schrecken.* Vienna and Leipzig: Internationaler Psychoanalytischer Verlag, 1929.

[97] The magical effects of interpretation described by Reik (for instance fright at the possibility that unconscious wishes might be fulfilled merely because the analyst gave expression to them) are to be interpreted as resistances.

[98] Reik, Theodor: *Surprise and the Psycho-Analyst.* New York: E. P. Dutton & Co., 1937.

[99] Alexander, Franz: *The Problem of Psychoanalytic Technique.* The Psa. Quarterly, IV, 1935. pp. 588–611.

Following a critical discussion of Ferenczi, Reich, and Kaiser, in which Reich is partly misunderstood and partly unconvincingly contradicted, Alexander emphasizes the confrontation of the ego with what was previously warded off as a partial manifestation of the 'synthetic function of the ego'. That 'today is not yesterday', the patient *learns* only through 'total' interpretations, as Alexander terms those interpretations which connect past experiences with present reality, so that the old material can now be coördinated in new contexts. That all this takes place mostly because dammed up instinctual energy becomes capable of discharge and the patient learns to get *satisfactions* is not worked out further.

Anna Freud's book, The Ego and the Mechanisms of Defense,[100] a fundamental work on the investigation of defense mechanisms and ego psychology in general, deals also with many problems of technique. We are shown how resistance analysis is necessary for true liberation of the forces bound up in the defense conflict. Her new insight into the dynamic and economic aspects of various defense mechanisms must naturally have a fertile effect upon the technique of influencing these defenses.

The proposals for an 'active technique' that originated with Ferenczi and his school, and the papers that have such proposals as their point of departure will not be discussed because we have already considered this subject in detail.

Since the end of 1936 when the lectures on which this discussion of the problems of psychoanalytic technique is based were concluded, problems of technique have frequently been discussed in the literature. Therefore it seems necessary to speak briefly at this point about at least three of these contributions that have appeared in the meantime. These are the symposium on The Theory of Therapeutic Results at the Fourteenth International Psychoanalytic Congress in Marienbad in August, 1936; a paper of Melitta Schmideberg, The

---

100 Freud, Anna: *The Ego and the Mechanisms of Defense.* London: Hogarth Press, 1936.

Mode of Operation of Psychoanalytic Therapy, and a paper, Analysis, Terminable and Interminable, in which Freud himself expresses some opinions about these questions.

The Marienbad symposium gives a clear picture of how far the opinions of analysts are still divergent over what really constitutes the effective factor in psychoanalytic therapy. An attempt at a complete and systematic exposition of the effective factors was undertaken by Bibring,[101] whose explanations in general coincide with our views.   He discusses the development of the changes which constitute the cure by taking up these processes from the respective points of view of the id, of the superego, and of the ego.

My own contribution [102] was identical with what I have expressed in section II of this volume.

Nunberg and Strachey discussed further what they had expressed in their earlier papers on the subject.   Nunberg [103] once more offered the opinion that abreaction (already effective in mere free association) and the synthetic function of the ego have the greatest significance as therapeutically effective factors. The tendency of the repressed to reach consciousness, he showed, is the force that aids us most in our therapeutic endeavors. He bases this upon the 'repetition compulsion' of which the transference is a special case. We should like however to express the opinion that when, after elimination of the defense, the energies of the warded off instincts accrue again to the disposal of the ego, the impetus to provide a discharge for what was warded off and therewith also the 'repetition compulsion' vanishes completely and is not merely 'drawn to the side of the ego'.   Strachey [104] held fast to his previous opinion that the essential task consists in making the superego more tolerant. This is done by means of correct 'transference interpretations', that is the interpretation of the feelings experi-

101 Bibring, Edward: *Symposium on the Theory of the Therapeutic Results of Psycho-Analysis*, VI. Int. J. Psa., XVIII, 1937. pp. 170–189.

102 Fenichel, Otto: *Ibid.*, pp. 133–138.

103 Nunberg, Hermann: *Ibid.*, pp. 161–169.

104 Strachey, James: *Ibid.*, pp. 139–145.

enced by the patient at the moment. In this the essential
point is the patient's 'introjection' of the analyst that takes
place at the moment of giving such an interpretation, in which
it is important 'that the patient shall introject [the analyst]
not as one more archaic imago added to the rest of the primitive superego, but as the nucleus of a separate and new
superego'.

Glover [105] expressed sceptical views about the possibility of
any theory of therapy at all: the actually effective factors are
extraordinarily diverse. While analytic 'interpretation' is
specially suited for the defense mechanism of repression
(hysteria), against other pathogenic mechanisms other therapeutic measures are effective. Among the latter a part is certainly played by mechanisms which in another degree and at
another point would themselves be pathogenic, such as displacements, introjections, projections.

Laforgue [106] designated as the two essential therapeutic
agents: (1) the patient's confidence in the physician, coinciding
with what we usually call 'suggestion', which in analysis however is used otherwise than in suggestion therapy, namely for
weakening the defenses and not for strengthening them;
(2) the patient's readiness for analytic work since he must
actively of his own volition work at the task of overcoming his
resistances. Determining factors for the magnitude of this
readiness for the analytic work are the wish for recovery and
occasionally the effects of certain shock experiences. Laforgue
then describes various types of greater or lesser will to recover
and discusses the rôle of the countertransference about which
we cannot agree with him that the analyst must be a 'leader'.
It is certainly true that there are patients who—particularly at
the beginning of an analysis—develop a 'magical' relationship
to the analyst which from the standpoint of therapy can be
curative to a certain degree, but which nevertheless becomes a
resistance and must be eliminated. I have not been able to

[105] Glover, Edward: *Ibid.*, pp. 125–132.
[106] Laforgue, René: *Der Heilungsfaktor der analytischen Behandlung.* Int.
Ztschr. Psa., XXIII, 1937. pp. 50–59.

convince myself either that 'magical transferences' are an indispensable requisite for analysis, or that they regularly exhibit a development parallel to the phylogenetic evolution of thinking.[107]

Bergler [108] emphasized that he wished not to present a theory of therapy but only to describe some factors that are effective in therapy. It strikes us that among these factors we find again some 'magical' ones which must of course be analyzed eventually as resistances. When a patient unconsciously looks upon psychoanalysis as sexual play and, fantasying that the analyst joins in this sexual play, draws the conclusion that his sexual fears were groundless, it would seem to me that a success based upon such a fantasy is a doubtful one and itself requires analysis. A sense of guilt stemming from infantile sexuality but displaced upon the question: 'Why do I not yet get well?' can certainly as a *vis a tergo* strengthen the will to recover in certain stages of an analysis. The displacement of the guilt feeling must however be reversed and the sense of guilt must again be connected with the infantile sexuality. Worthy of attention is what Bergler calls 'the unconscious resonance of the physician's consistency'. He writes (pp. 152–153): 'At the beginning of analysis our interpretations strike our patients as completely absurd and they constantly counter them with logical arguments. From the exalted pinnacles of logic and common sense, they look down upon us compassionately, ironically and sometimes actually in despair of our intelligence. . . . The only thing which takes them aback is the consistency with which we defend our point of view. . . . It is a fact of experience that in life in general any assertion

[107] Laforgue writes (*loc. cit.*, p. 59) : 'The infantile oral-anal ego of the neurotic seeks with the help of the analyst to master anxiety and reality at first by means of magic and makes of the analyst a magician. Later the anxiety can be mastered and the attempt is made to attain adaptation to reality on a religious level. In this the analyst assumes the rôle of a leader. Finally, in a later stage of the treatment, the patient attempts to identify himself with the analyst.'

[108] Bergler, Edmund: *Symposium on the Theory of the Therapeutic Results of Psycho-Analysis*, IV. Int. J. Psa., XVIII, 1937. pp. 146–160.

which is made with inner conviction, however absurd it may
be, is disconcerting. The most superficial explanation is that
opinions, expressed unwaveringly and with inner conviction,
have the effect of a challenge to the scepticism of the hearer.
Since all patients are consumed with internal ambivalence, the
analyst's consistency *eo ipso* undermines their doubts. As far
as the internal truth of our statements is concerned, they are
quite incapable of forming a judgment at the beginning of the
treatment.' Even beyond this the consistency of the physician
is supposed by Bergler to have therapeutically valuable effects
in other respects as well. The quotation from Bergler shows
that he has an understanding of 'interpretation' quite different
from ours. We consider it a mistake to have analytic interpretations at the beginning of the treatment make upon the
patient an impression of complete absurdity, and we consider it correct at the beginning of the treatment to make to
patients only such assertions whose internal truth they are
completely capable of judging.

The paper of Melitta Schmideberg [109] brings together several
of her other contributions.[110] As an auxiliary force supporting
the efforts of the analyst to induce his patient to give free associations, there comes into question according to Schmideberg not
only the impetus of the repressed towards motility, but also 'the
wish to give something good to the people one loves', the
'reparation tendency'. Interpretations make the exertion of
resistance superfluous and thus support the natural tendency
toward 'synthesis'. Making the unconscious conscious nor-
mally comes about through interpretation with the aid of inter-
posing of preconscious ideas, a process we have called 'confrontation of the ego with the previously unconscious contents'.
Schmideberg believes however that it can occasionally take

[109] Schmideberg, Melitta: *The Mode of Operation of Psycho-Analytic
Therapy.* Int. J. Psa., XIX, 1938. pp. 310–321.
[110] Schmideberg, Melitta: *Zur Wirkungsweise der psychoanalytischen
Therapie.* Int. Ztschr. Psa., XXI, 1935. pp. 46–54. *Reassurance as a Means of
Analytic Technique.* Int. J. Psa., XVI, 1935. pp. 307–324. *After the Analysis.*
The Psa. Quarterly, VII, 1938. pp. 122–143.

place without such an intermediary stage. She writes [111]: 'Emotions constitute one direct link between consciousness and the unconscious and symbolism is another. For this reason, symbolic interpretations which are associated with feelings offer a direct approach to the unconscious, and are especially valuable with patients in whom the preconscious has only developed imperfectly (young children, psychotics).'

This seems to us doubtful. In the description of the changes which take place during analysis in the instinctual structure of the patients, Schmideberg does not mention the significance of the fact that after elimination of repressions, the libido previously bound to infantile aims is subjected to the primacy of the genital and therefore becomes capable of satisfaction. The following seems to her more essential (p. 315): 'Analysis effects a new and improved fusion of the impulses liberated as a result of transitory defusion, and consequently a modification of the original impulses: aggressive impulses are libidinized and sexual ones more elaborately distributed, i.e., sublimated. The aggression liberated in analysis is extensively employed in the work of organizing the id. Sexual fixations are loosened as a consequence of the reduction and more advantageous distribution of the underlying anxiety and aggression.' She too emphasizes that in practice in addition to these measures specific for analysis other unspecific ones also have therapeutic effect.

It is impossible in a few sentences to do justice to the thirty-three pages, so rich in meaning, of Freud's paper, Analysis Terminable and Interminable.[112] Only a few things particularly important for our subject may be given special attention. Freud writes (p. 377): 'Instead of inquiring *how* analysis effects a cure (a point which in my opinion has been sufficiently elucidated) we should ask what are the obstacles which this cure encounters'. Accordingly his paper examines

111 Schmideberg, Melitta: *The Mode of Operation of Psycho-Analytic Therapy. Loc cit.*

112 Freud: *Analysis Terminable and Interminable.* Int. J. Psa., XVIII, 1937. pp. 373–405.

these obstacles. To be sure our comprehension of the problems of the failures of analysis depends upon the 'sufficient
elucidation' of the success in other cases. The evident differences between the views of the authors of the Marienbad symposium seem to show that even in the matter of
the success of analysis much is not yet clear to the analysts'
comprehension.

At any rate, Freud examines the 'obstacles' in a discussion
of the effects of traumas, of absolute and relative strength of
instincts, and of ego modifications that make analysis more
difficult. The problem of *shortening* the treatment, which is
his point of departure, soon gives way to another problem.
Rank's attempt to shorten treatment was, like many others,
completely unsatisfactory; and fixing a date for concluding
analysis, sometimes necessary for compulsion neurotics, is
essentially a two-edged measure. We would gladly take long
periods of time if we were only sure of attaining our goal.
What is the goal? Must we require assurance against future
relapses? Freud believes that the optimistic point of view
implied in the very question of the avoidability of relapses pre-
supposes 'a number of things which are not exactly a matter
of course', and these presuppositions are (p. 380): 'in the first
place, . . . that it is really possible to resolve an instinctual
conflict (or, more accurately, a conflict between the ego and an
instinct) finally and for all time; secondly, that when we are
dealing with one such conflict in a patient, we can, as it were,
inoculate him against the possibility of any other instinctual
conflicts in the future; and thirdly, that we have the power,
for purposes of prophylaxis, to stir up a pathogenic conflict of
this sort, when at the moment there is no indication of it. . . .'
Perhaps, however, these presuppositions are not so completely
unjustified, as our discussion of Freud's following arguments
will attempt to show.

Freud's remarks about the strength of instincts as an obstacle
to therapy we would supplement by referring to the physiological periodicity of the strength of instinct. Instincts only
become insuperably strong when they are shut off from dis-

charge and are thus dammed up. Freud explains (p. 381) the concept of 'permanent settlement of an instinctual claim' as follows: 'That is to say, it is brought into harmony with the ego and becomes accessible to the influence of the other ego-tendencies, no longer seeking for independent gratification'. However, just that sort of settlement of an instinctual claim succeeds the less, the more dammed back the instinct is. Only when the instinct, barred from motility and from the ego, must carry on its existence in the unconscious, repeatedly producing and sending out from there derivatives at the wrong point and the wrong time—it is only then that the instinct is so completely subject to the primary process that it evades all restraint. Certainly 'permanent settlement of an instinctual claim' cannot mean causing it to vanish completely. What it must mean is that the possibility should be provided of avoiding instinctual damming up by virtue of the discharge of the greater part of the instinctual energy. Then the remaining instinctual claims requiring suppression are relatively lacking in energy content. The point is to regulate quantitatively the relation between instinct that impels to action and ego which carries out actions. It is thus a question less of the absolute than of the relative strength of instinct (which is diminished by satisfaction and therefore indirectly by psychoanalysis) which makes satisfaction possible.

The prerequisite for such psychoanalytic success would seem to be that the analysis be carried out correctly in its economic aspect. Since it is not possible, as Freud makes clear, to settle completely in analysis *all* unsettled remainders from the past, the point is that the *more essential part* of the remainders should be settled. For this purpose, in all cases in which unsettled remainders of the past (containing the threat of relapses) are solidified in relatively constant structures such as character attitudes, it would seem necessary to attack and to dissolve these solidified structures at the very beginning.

All this seems to be contradicted when we read in Freud's paper (p. 386) that for the purpose of guarding a patient against future instinctual conflicts we have to turn 'a possible

future conflict into a present one . . .', and this cannot be
done. 'Tempting as it may be to our therapeutic ambition to
propose such tasks for itself, experience bids us refuse them out
of hand'; for in order to transform a latent instinctual conflict
into a present one, 'there are only two things we can do: either
we can bring about situations in which the conflict becomes
actual or we can content ourselves with discussing it in
analysis. . . .' The former we do not attempt, for 'to conjure
up fresh suffering [is] a thing which we have so far rightly left
to fate'. The latter does not work because merely talking
about something cannot really settle it.

This much is clear. The question arises however as to
whether these are really the only two possibilities. It is certainly not a question of creating fresh conflicts that are not
present, but of mobilizing latent ones. Never are these conflicts
completely dormant; the ego merely acts as if they were. The
analyst is accustomed to detecting great conflicts behind the
smallest signs. His task then is to make clear to the patient the
actuality of the 'conflict', in other words to put the patient's ego
at a distance from these signs, so that the rationalizations, eruptions and derivatives become noticeable to the ego. Of what
use is it to discuss with the patient only those matters that
occupy him consciously if one at the same time overlooks the
fact that at certain points where the patient himself feels no
conflict alive within him, the energies which made him ill are
'tonically' bound in a way unknown to him? We must then, it
seems to me, literally 'transform a latent instinctual conflict into
a present one' if we wish to resolve it, to render capable of discharge the decisive portion of the solidified instinctual energy
bound in it, and so to restore health. Thus we must 'bring
about situations in which the conflict becomes actual'. We do
this however not by imitating fate with interference in the
patient's real life nor by joining artificially in the play of the
transference, but by psychoanalysis of those points at which
the latent conflicts make themselves evident by naming their
derivatives and inducing the observing ego to stand at a
'distance' from them.

I should like to call special attention to one more sentence (p. 387) from this context: 'The work of analysis progresses best when the patient's pathogenic experiences belong to the past so that the ego can stand at a distance from them.' That is certainly an important warning to the partisans of acting out and of 'affective eruptions'. But there is a special circumstance about this 'distance' of the ego. Distance can be established with respect to latent conflicts only if it is first temporarily diminished or abolished. It should never become so great that the patient's feeling, 'This matter concerns me', or 'I must occupy myself with my past because it interferes disturbingly in the present', is replaced by the opposite feeling, 'About all this I can talk quite comfortably, for I stand at a distance from it, and it does not concern me any longer'.

In his discussion of problems of *ego modifications* that make analysis more difficult, Freud reminds us first of the fact that for analytic work we need the patient's reasonable ego. Our work rests upon its coöperation, and in his very earliest recommendations on technique [113] Freud considered its intactness an absolute prerequisite for the successful accomplishment of an analysis. Now it turns out that only in the fewest cases is the ego intact. There can also be, as Freud notes, constitutional peculiarities of the ego which make analysis more difficult. As a rule, however, the fact is that infantile instinctual conflicts have produced in the structure and modes of function of the ego, alterations which either appear only in certain situations (phobic attitudes and their further developments) or are solidified as 'character attitudes' and reactive peculiarities. With these it is a matter of defensive functions not adapted to the present situation but which set in automatically and are broken through by unrecognized escape-eruptions of instincts; and all this corresponds to the fact that by virtue of the defense itself the domain in question is withheld from further development. By force of circumstance, psychoanalysis has long been

[113] Freud: *On Psychotherapy* (1904). Coll. Papers, Vol. I. London: Hogarth Press, 1924. pp. 257–258.

interested in these problems of 'character analysis'. We know essentially how to attack the problem: we split the ego, so to speak. To its residual reasonable, observing portion we demonstrate its behavior, show the behavior to be produced purposefully by the ego, discover the purpose and trace it finally to its historical origin—nothing different from what we do with symptoms which are more a distorted expression of the id. Freud is sceptical about the therapeutic expectations from the 'historical reduction' of ego modifications. The ego under the influence of education has accustomed itself, says Freud, to displacing the scene of conflict from without to within; then, unable to become free of the ghosts it has conjured up, frequently calls them up at points where they are disturbing, in the analysis itself as well. Freud nevertheless admits (p. 393): 'This must not be taken to imply that they [defensive ego modifications] make analysis impossible. On the contrary, they constitute half of our analytic task.' However, this half of the work is very difficult. While the warded off instinct is our ally in the analytic work, the defensive part of the ego is our adversary, since it is only interested in maintaining the resistances; and the reasonable ego, which could aid us, is at first powerless against this defensive portion of the ego. It is the essence of resistance that it does not allow itself to be revealed without further resistance.

Again, whether or not we can master these difficulties depends upon quantitative relationships. Further, there must be taken into account (p. 395) what Freud in The Problem of Anxiety designated as 'resistance of the id'.[114] Many persons seem to have such an 'adhesiveness' of their libido that they cannot be dislodged from a customary mode of behavior. Others are easily changed, but the changes produced are evanescent, and 'one feels not as if one had worked in clay but as if one had written in water'.

Freud believes (pp. 396–398) that to all these difficulties in dealing with ego modifications a further one is added which

114 Freud: *The Problem of Anxiety*. New York: The Psa. Quarterly Press and W. W. Norton & Co., Inc., 1936. pp. 137–139.

he derives from his conception of the biological genuineness of the destructive instinct. Some persons who at the same time have instincts with contradictory aims, tranquilly allow these contradictory tendencies to exist one next to the other or one after the other without being particularly affected. Others suffer from this contradiction, and it becomes for them a severe psychic conflict which they try to settle by erecting a defense against one of the two conflicting instincts. This 'inclination to conflict' in many people which enormously increases the difficulty of their analysis, Freud would trace to a constitutionally determined higher quantum of 'free floating destructive energy'. But, we may ask, does not the explanation suffice that in those cases in which the contradictions between instincts are experienced as severe conflicts, it regularly turns out that one of the conflicting instincts is relatively more ego-syntonic, the other relatively more warded off? A greater inclination to conflict is possessed by those individuals whose instinctual conflict expresses in addition a 'structural' conflict. Since persons who have more structural conflicts are those who have turned one part of their instinctual energies against the self in such a way that they now serve for the suppression of other instinctual claims, it is understandable that these same persons with greater inclination to conflicts also evidence more inclination to self-destruction.

Freud's noteworthy discussion of the psychology of the analyst needs no further mention here. The concluding section of his paper holds that we approach with greatest difficulty those resistances that extend into the biological sphere, and by that he means bisexuality. In both man and woman the impulses proper to the opposite sex incur repression. The man's rejection of his passive homosexual femininity and the woman's of her masculine wish for a penis constitute the obstacles to therapeutic success most difficult to remove. To be sure, the two are not quite analogous according to Freud's discussion. For the man the difficulty comes from clinging to his *fear* of being feminine. He cannot assume the passive attitude because it unconsciously signifies for him the dreaded castration. For the woman the difficulty comes from clinging to her *pleasure* in being masculine. She cannot assume the required passive attitudes because she would prefer to be active. This distinction seems highly significant. Perhaps there lies in it an indication that we should be wary of reaching back to biology as long as experiential and social factors can still be operative. Some of our women patients, Freud states, because of their penis envy consider analysis of no avail. 'We can only agree with them', he writes (p. 405), 'when we discover that their strongest motive in coming for treatment was the hope that they might somehow still obtain a male organ, the lack of which is so painful to them'. But what brings most patients into analysis is the hope for fulfilment of old libidinal and hostile (revenge) infantile impulses, the hope for better crutches rather than the hope of attaining a state in which crutches are superfluous. Penis envy in this connection does not seem to possess any essential uniqueness. We must in analysis make efforts to see through every type of 'unconscious wish for recovery' as early as possible in order to eliminate this abundant source of resistances. It is true that these efforts especially often fail in instances of castration anxiety in men and of penis envy in women.

BIBLIOGRAPHY

1. ABRAHAM, KARL.: *Sollen wir die Patienten ihre Träume aufschreiben lassen?* Int. Ztschr. Psa., I, 1913, pp. 194–196.
2. ————— A Particular Form of Neurotic Resistance Against the Psycho-Analytic Method, in his *Selected Papers*. London: Hogarth Press, 1927.
3. ————— The Applicability of Psycho-Analytic Treatment to Patients at an Advanced Age, in his *Selected Papers*. London: Hogarth Press, 1927.
4. ————— *Psycho-Analytical Notes on Coués Method of Self-Mastery.* Int. J. Psa., VII, 1926, pp. 190–213.
5. ALEXANDER, FRANZ: *A Metapsychological Description of the Process of Cure.* Int. J. Psa., VI, 1925, pp. 13–34.
6. ————— *Psychoanalysis of the Total Personality.* London: Hogarth Press, 1927.
7. ————— *Der neurotische Charakter.* Int. Ztschr. Psa., XIV, 1928, pp. 26–44.
8. ————— *On Ferenczi's 'Relaxation Principle'.* Int. J Psa., XIV, 1933, pp. 183–192.
9. ————— *The Relation of Structural and Instinctual Conflicts.* The Psa. Quarterly, II, 1933, pp. 181–207.
10. ————— *The Problem of Psychoanalytic Technique.* The Psa. Quarterly, IV, 1935, pp. 588–611.
11. ————— Review of Kubie: *'Practical Aspects of Psychoanalysis'.* The Psa. Quarterly, V, 1936, pp. 283–289.
12. BALINT, ALICE: *Handhabung der Übertragung auf Grund der Ferenczischen Versuche.* Int. Ztschr. Psa., XXII, 1936, pp. 47–58.
13. BÁLINT, MICHAEL: *Charakter und Neubeginn.* Int. Ztschr. Psa., XX, 1934, pp. 54–65.
14. ————— *The Final Goal of Psychoanalytic Treatment.* Int. J. Psa., XVII, 1936, pp. 206–216.
15. BEHN-ESCHENBURG, HANS: *Über eine seltene Deutung des Widerstandes.* Int. Ztschr. Psa., XVII, 1931, pp. 276–282.
16. BENEDEK, THERESE: *Defense Mechanisms and Structure of the Total Personality.* The Psa. Quarterly, VI, 1937, pp. 96–118.
17. BERGLER, EDMUND: *Symposium on the Theory of Therapeutic Results of Psychoanalysis.* Int. J. Psa., XVIII, 1937, pp. 146–161.
18. BERNFELD, SIEFRIED: *Der Begriff der Deutung in der Psychoanalyse.* Ztschr. f. angew. Psychol., XLII, 1932, pp. 448–497.
19. BIBRING, EDUARD: *Symposium on the Theory of Therapeutic Results of Psychoanalysis.* Int. J. Psa., XVIII, 1937, pp. 170–189.
20. BIBRING-LEHNER, GRETE: *A Contribution to the Subject of Transference Resistance.* Int. J. Psa., XVII, 1936, pp. 181–189.
21. BLEULER, EUGEN: *Das autistisch undisziplinierte Denken in der Medizin.* Berlin: Springer, 1927.
22. BOEHM, FELIX: *Dürfen wir Gefälligkeiten von Patienten annehmen?* Int. Ztschr. Psa., IX, 1923, p. 77.
23. ————— *Das Unbewusste des Analytikers in der Analyse.* Int. Ztschr. Psa., IX, 1923, pp. 77–78.

24. BREUER, JOSEF, AND FREUD: *Studien über Hysterie*. Leipzig and Vienna: Franz Deuticke, 1895.

25. BRILL, A. A.: *A Few Remarks on the Technique of Psychoanalysis*. Med. Rev. of Rev., April, 1912.

26. ——— *Psychoanalysis: Its Theories and Practical Application*. Philadelphia and London: W. B. Saunders Co., 1913.

27. BUNKER, HENRY A.: Psychotherapy and Psychoanalysis, in Lorand's *Psychoanalysis Today: Its Scope and Function*. New York: Covici Friede, Inc., 1933.

28. CARNCROSS, H.: *Activity in Analysis*. Psa. Rev., XIII, 1926, pp. 281–293.

29. CLARK, L. PIERCE: *Some Practical Remarks upon the Use of Modified Psychoanalysis in the Treatment of Borderland Neuroses and Psychoses*. Psa. Rev., VI, 1919, pp. 306–308.

30. COLE, E. M.: *A Few 'Dont's' for Beginners in the Technique of Psychoanalysis*. Int. J. Psa., III, 1922, pp. 43–44.

31. CORIAT, ISADOR H.: *Some Statistical Results of the Psychoanalytic Treatment of the Psycho-Neuroses*. Psa. Rev., IV, 1917, pp. 209–216.

32. ——— *Active Therapy in Psychoanalysis*. Psa. Rev., XI, 1924, pp. 28–38.

33. DEUTSCH, HELENE.: *Psychoanalysis of the Neuroses*. London: Hogarth Press, 1933.

34. EDER, M. D.: *Dreams as Resistance*. Int. J. Psa., XI, 1930, pp. 40–47.

35. EITINGTON, MAX: *Reminiszenzen aus der Geschichte der Psychotherapie*. Int. Ztschr. Psa., XVI, 1930, pp. 165–171.

36. ——— *Über neuere Methoden-Kritik an der Psychoanalyse*. Int. Ztschr. Psa., XVII, 1931, pp. 5–15.

37. FARROW, E. PICKWORTH: *A Method of Self-Analysis*. Brit. J. of Med. Psychol., V, 1925, pp. 106–118.

38. FENICHEL, OTTO: *Outline of Clinical Psychoanalysis*. New York: The Psa. Quarterly Press and W. W. Norton and Co., 1932.

39. ——— *Zur Theorie der psychoanalytischen Technik*. Int. Ztschr. Psa., XXI, 1935, pp. 78–95.

40. ——— *Symposium on the Theory of Therapeutic Results of Psychoanalysis*. Int. J. Psa., XVIII, 1937, pp. 133–139.

41. ——— *Ego Disturbances and Their Treatment*. Int. J. Psa., XIX, 1938, pp. 416–438.

42. FERENCZI, SANDOR: Introjection and Transference, in *Contributions to Psychoanalysis*. Boston: Richard G. Badger, 1916.

43. ——— A Transitory Symptom: The Position During Treatment, in *Further Contributions to the Theory and Technique of Psychoanalysis*. London: Institute of Psycho-Analysis and Hogarth Press, 1926.

44. ——— On the Feeling of Giddiness at the End of the Analytical Hour, *Ibid*.

45. ——— Falling Asleep During the Analysis, *Ibid*.

46. ——— Discontinuous Analysis, *Ibid*.

47. ——— Restlessness Towards the End of the Hour of Analysis, *Ibid*.

48. ——— Technical Difficulties in an Analysis of Hysteria, *Ibid*.

49. ——— On the Technique of Psycho-Analysis, *Ibid*.

50. ——— On Influencing the Patient in Psychoanalysis, *Ibid*.

51. ———— Further Developments of 'Active' Technique, *Ibid.*

52. ———— AND RANK, OTTO: *The Development of Psychoanalysis.* Nerv. and Ment. Dis. Pub. Co., Monograph Series, No. 40, 1925.

53. ———— On Forced Phantasies, in *Further Contributions to the Theory and Technique of Psychoanalysis.* London: Institute of Psycho-Analysis and Hogarth Press, 1926.

54. ———— Psychoanalysis of Sexual Habits, *Ibid.*

55. ———— Contraindications to the Active Psychoanalytical Technique, *Ibid.*

56. ———— *Zur Kritik der Rank'schen Technik der Psychoanalyse.* Int. Ztschr. Psa., XIII, 1927, pp. 1–9.

57. ———— *Das Problem der Beendigung der Analysen.* Int. Ztschr. Psa., XIV, 1928, pp. 1–10.

58. ———— *Die Elastizität der psychoanalytischen Technik.* Int. Ztschr. Psa., XIV, 1928, pp. 197–209.

59. ———— *The Principle of Relaxation and Neocatharsis.* Int. J. Psa., XI, 1930, pp. 428–443.

60. ———— *Child Analysis in the Analysis of Adults.* Int. J. Psa., XII, 1931, pp. 468–482.

61. ———— *Sprachverwirrung zwischen dem Erwachsenen und dem Kinde.* Int. Ztschr. Psa., XIX, 1933, pp. 5–15.

62. FORSYTH, DAVID: *The Technique of Psychoanalysis.* London: Kegan Paul, Ltd., 1933.

63. FRENCH, THOMAS M.: *A Clinical Study of Learning in the Course of a Psychoanalytic Treatment.* The Psa. Quarterly, V, 1936, pp. 148–194.

64. FREUD, ANNA: *The Technique of Child-Analysis.* New York and Washington: Nerv. and Ment. Dis. Pub. Co., 1928.

65. ———— *The Ego and the Mechanisms of Defense.* London: Hogarth Press, 1937.

66. FREUD: *The Interpretation of Dreams.* London: Allen and Unwin, 1915.

67. ———— *Freud's Psycho-Analytic Method.* Coll. Papers, I.

68. ———— *Three Contributions to the Theory of Sex.* New York: Nerv. and Ment. Dis. Pub. Co., 1910.

69. ———— *Wit and Its Relation to the Unconscious.* London: Fisher Unwin, 1916.

70. ———— *Fragment of an Analysis of a Case of Hysteria.* Coll. Papers, III.

71. ———— *Analysis of a Phobia in a Five-year-old Boy.* Coll. Papers, III.

72. ———— *Notes upon a Case of Obsessional Neuroses.* Coll Papers, III.

73. ———— *On Psychoanalysis.* Amer. J. of Psychol., 1910.

74. ———— *The Future Prospects of Psycho-Analytic Therapy.* Coll. Papers, II.

75. ———— *Observations on 'Wild' Psycho-Analysis.* Coll. Papers, II.

76. ———— *The Employment of Dream-Interpretation in Psycho-Analysis.* Coll. Papers, II.

77. ———— *The Dynamics of the Transference.* Coll. Papers, II.

78. ———— *Recommendations for Physicians on the Psycho-Analytic Method of Treatment.* Coll. Papers, II.

79. ———— *Fausse Reconnaissance ('Déjà Raconté') in Psycho-Analytic Treatment.* Coll. Papers, II.

80. ——— *Further Recommendations in the Technique of Psycho-Analysis.* Coll. Papers, II.

81. ——— *On Narcissism: An Introduction.* Coll. Papers, IV.

82. ——— *The Unconscious.* Coll. Papers, IV.

83. ——— *Some Character-Types Met with in Psycho-Analytic Work.* Coll. Papers, IV.

84. ——— *A General Introduction to Psychoanalysis.* New York: Liveright Publishing Corp., 1935.

85. ——— *Mourning and Melancholia.* Coll. Papers, IV.

86. ——— *From the History of an Infantile Neurosis.* Coll. Papers, III.

87. ——— *Turnings in the Ways of Psycho-Analytic Therapy.* Coll. Papers, II.

88. ——— Introduction to *Psychoanalysis and the War Neuroses.* London: Int. Psa. Press, 1921.

89. ——— *Zur Vorgeschichte der analytischen Technik.* Int. Ztschr. Psa., VI, 1920, pp. 79–81.

90. ——— *The Psychogenesis of a Case of Homosexuality in a Woman.* Coll. Papers, II.

91. ——— *Beyond the Pleasure Principle.* London: Int. Psa. Press, 1922.

92. ——— *Group Psychology and the Analysis of the Ego.* Vienna: Int. Psa. Verlag, 1922.

93. ——— *The Ego and the Id.* London: Institute of Psycho-Analysis and Hogarth Press 1927.

94. ——— *Bemerkungen zur Theorie und Praxis der Traumdeutung.* Ges. Schr., III.

95. ——— *The Problem of Anxiety.* New York: The Psa. Quarterly Press and W. W. Norton & Co., 1936.

96. ——— *New Introductory Lectures on Psychoanalysis.* London: Hogarth Press, 1933.

97. ——— *Analysis Terminable and Interminable.* Int. J. Psa., XVIII, 1937, pp. 373–405.

98. ——— *Constructions in Analysis.* Int. J. Psa., XIX, 1938, pp. 377–387.

99. FUCHS, S. H.: *Zum Stand der heutigen Biologie.* Imago, XXII, 1936, pp. 210–241.

100. GLOVER, EDWARD: *'Active Therapy' and Psycho-Analysis.* Int. J. Psa., V, 1924, pp. 269–311.

01. ——— *Critical Notice of 'Entwicklungsziele der Psychoanalyse' von S. Ferenczi und Otto Rank.* Brit. J. of Med. Psychol., IV, 1924, pp. 319–325.

102. ——— *A 'Technical' Form of Resistance.* Int. J. Psa., VII, 1926, pp. 377–380.

103. ——— *Lectures on Technique in Psycho-Analysis.* Int. J. Psa., VIII, 1927, pp. 311–338, 486–520; IX, 1928, pp. 7–46, 181–218.

104. ——— *The Vehicle of Interpretations.* Int. J. Psa., XI, 1930, pp. 340–344.

105. ——— *The Therapeutic Effect of Inexact Interpretation.* Int. J. Psa., XII, 1931, pp. 397–411.

06. ——— *Symposium on the Theory of Therapeutic Results of Psycho-Analysis.* Int. J. Psa., XVIII, 1937, pp. 125–133.

107. HANN-KENDE, FANNY: *Zur Übertragung und Gegenübertragung in der Psychoanalyse.* Int. Ztschr. Psa., XII, 1926, pp. 478–486.

108. HÁRNIK, J.: *Über die Forcierung blasphemischer Fantasien.* Int. Ztschr. Psa., XIII, 1927, pp. 61–64.

109. —— *Resistance to the Interpretation of Dreams in Analysis.* Int. J. Psa., XI, 1930, pp. 75–78.

110. HARTMANN, HEINZ: *Die Grundlagen der Psychoanalyse.* Leipzig: Georg Thieme, 1927.

111. HENDRICK, IVES: *Facts and Theories of Psychoanalysis.* New York: Alfred A. Knopf, 1934.

112. HERMANN, IMRE: *Die Psychoanalyse als Methode.* Vienna: Int. Psa. Verlag, 1934.

113. HITSCHMANN, EDUARD: *Die Indikationen für psychoanalytische Behandlung.* Vienna: Ars Medici, XIV, No. 10, 1924.

114. —— *Wandlungen der Traum-Symbolik beim Fortschreiten der Behandlung.* Int. Ztschr. Psa., XVII, 1931, pp. 140–142.

115. HORNEY, KAREN: *Die Technik der psychoanalytischen Therapie.* Ztschr. f. Sexualwissenschaft, IV, 1917, p. 185 ff.

116. —— *The Problem of the Negative Therapeutic Reaction.* The Psa. Quarterly, V, 1936, pp. 29–44.

117. JEKELS, LUDWIG, AND BERGLER, EDMUND: *Übertragung und Liebe.* Imago, XX, 1934, pp. 5–31.

118. JELLIFFE, SMITH ELY: *The Technique of Psychoanalysis.* New York: Nerv. and Ment. Dis. Pub. Co., Monograph Series, No. 26, 1914.

119. —— *Some Notes on Transference.* J. Abnormal Psychol., VIII, No. 5, 1914, p. 302.

120. —— *Contributions to Psychotherapeutic Technique through Psychoanalysis.* Psa. Rev., VI, 1919, pp. 1–14.

121. —— *The Old Age Factor in Psychoanalytical Therapy.* Med. J. and Record, New York, No. 1, 1925.

122. JONES, ERNEST: The Psycho-Analytic Method of Treatment in *Papers on Psycho-Analysis.* Baltimore: Wm. Wood and Co.; London: Bailliere, Tindall and Cox, 1913.

123. —— Psycho-Analysis in Psychotherapy, *Ibid.*

124. —— Reflections on Some Criticisms of the Psycho-Analytic Method of Treatment, *Ibid.*

125. —— The Attitude of the Psycho-Analytic Physician Towards Current Conflicts, *Ibid.*

126. —— *Die Technik der Psychoanalytischen Therapie.* Jahrb. f. psa. Forschungen, VI, July, 1914, pp. 329–342.

127. —— Some Practical Aspects of the Psycho-Analytic Treatment, in *Papers on Psycho-Analysis.* Baltimore: Wm. Wood and Co.; London: Bailliere, Tindall and Cox, 1913.

128. —— *Bemerkungen zur psychoanalytischen Technik. I. Träume in der Psychoanalyse. II. Suggestion and Übertragung.* Int. Ztschr. Psa., II. 1914, pp. 274–275.

129. —— *Treatment of the Neuroses.* Baltimore: Wm. Wood. and Co.; London: Bailliere, Tindall and Cox, 1920.

130. ———— The Nature of Auto-Suggestion, in *Papers on Psycho-Analysis.* Baltimore: Wm. Wood and Co.; London: Bailliere, Tindall and Cox, 1913.

131. ———— *Theorie und Praxis in der Psychoanalyse.* Int. Ztschr. Psa., XI, 1925, pp. 145–149.

132. KAISER, HELMUTH: *Probleme der Technik.* Int. Ztschr. Psa., XX, 1934, pp. 490–522.

133. KLEIN, MELANIE: *The Psychoanalysis of Children.* London: Hogarth Press, 1932.

134. KOVÁCS, VILMA: *Beispiele zur aktiven Technik.* Int. Ztschr. Psa., XIV, 1928, pp. 405–408.

135. ———— *Training- and Control-Analysis.* Int. J. Psa., XVII, 1936, pp. 346–354.

136. KUBIE, LAWRENCE S.: *Über die Beziehung zwischen dem bedingten Reflex und der psychoanalytischen Technik.* Imago, XXI, 1935, pp. 44–50.

137. ———— *Practical Aspects of Psychoanalysis.* New York: W. W. Norton and Co., 1936.

138. LAFORGUE, RENÉ: *'Active' Psychoanalytical Technique and the Will to Recovery.* Int. J. Psa., X, 1929, pp. 411–422.

139. ———— *Resistances at the Conclusion of Analytical Treatment.* Int. J. Psa., XV, 1934, pp. 419–434.

140. ———— *Exceptions to the Fundamental Rule.* The Psa. Quarterly, V, 1936, pp. 369–374.

141. ———— *Der Heilungsfaktor der analytischen Behandlung.* Int. Ztschr. Psa., XXIII, 1937, pp. 50–59.

142. LANDAUER, CARL: *'Passive' Technik.* Int. Ztschr. Psa., X, 1924, pp. 415–422.

143. LOEWENSTEIN, RUDOLF: *Bemerkungen zur Theorie des therapeutischen Vorganges der Psychoanalyse.* Int. Ztschr. Psa., XXIII, 1937, pp. 560–563.

144. LOW, BARBARA: *Psychoanalysis: A Brief Account of the Freudian Theory.* London: George Allen and Unwin, Ltd., 1920.

145. ———— *The Psychological Compensations of the Analyst.* Int. J. Psa., XVI, 1935, pp. 1–8.

146. MACK BRUNSWICK, RUTH: *A Supplement to Freud's 'History of an Infantile Neurosis'.* Int. J. Psa., IX, 1928, pp. 439–476.

147. MUELLER-BRAUNSCHWEIG, CARL: *Der psychoanalytische Prozess.* Ztschr. f. Sexualwissenschaft, IX, 1923, pp. 301–310.

148. NUNBERG, HERMANN: *The Will to Recovery.* Int. J. Psa., VII, 1926, pp. 64–78.

149. ———— *Probleme der Therapie.* Int. Ztschr. Psa., XIV, 1928, p. 441 ff.

150. ———— *The Synthetic Function of the Ego.* Int. J. Psa., XII, 1931, p. 123 ff.

151. ———— *Allgemeine Neurosenlehre auf psychoanalytischer Grundlage.* Berne: Hans Huber, 1932.

152. ———— The Theoretical Basis of Psychoanalytic Therapy, in Lorand's *Psychoanalysis Today: Its Scope and Function.* New York: Covici Friede, Inc., 1931.

153. ——— Symposium on the Theory of Therapeutic Results of Psycho-Analysis. Int. J. Psa., XVIII, 1937, pp. 161–170.

154. OBERNDORF, C. P.: The Scope and Technique of Psychoanalysis. Med. Record, Nov. 22, 1912.

155. ——— The Practice of Psychoanalysis. N. Y. State J. of Med., XXI, 1921, p. 95.

156. ——— Technical Procedure in the Analytic Treatment of Children. Int. J. Psa., XI, 1930, pp. 79–82.

157. RADO, SANDOR: The Economic Principle in Psycho-Analytic Technique. Int. J. Psa., VI, 1925, pp. 35–44.

158. RANK, OTTO: Zum Verständnis der Libidoentwicklung im Heilungsvorgang. Int. Ztschr. Psa., IX, 1923, pp. 435–471.

159. ——— The Trauma of Birth and Its Importance for Psychoanalytic Therapy. New York: Harcourt, Brace and Co., 1924.

160. ——— Technik der Psychoanalyse. Vienna and Leipzig: Franz Deuticke, 1926.

161. REICH, WILHELM: Zwei narzisstische Typen. Int. Ztschr. Psa., VIII, 1922, pp. 456–462.

162. ——— Der triebhafte Charakter. Neue Arbeiten z. aerztl. Psychoanalyse, No. 4, Vienna: Int. Psa. Verlag, 1925.

163. ——— Weitere Bemerkungen über die therapeutische Bedeutung der Genitallibido. Int. Ztschr. Psa., XI, 1925, pp. 297–317.

164. ——— Zur Technik der Deutung und der Widerstandsanalyse. Int. Ztschr. Psa., XIII, 1927, pp. 141–159.

165. ——— Über Charakter-Analyse. Int. Ztschr. Psa., XIV, 1928, pp. 180–196.

166. ——— Charakter-Analyse. Technik und Grundlagen, published by the author in Vienna, 1933.

167. ——— Psychischer Kontakt und vegetative Strömung. Copenhagen: Sexpol-Verlag, 1935.

168. REIK, THEODOR: Some Remarks on the Study of Resistances. Int. J. Psa., V, 1924, pp. 141–154.

169. ——— The Therapy of the Neuroses and Religion. Int. J. Psa., X, 1929, pp. 292–302.

170. ——— New Ways in Psycho-Analytic Technique. Int. J. Psa., XIV, 1933, pp. 321–334.

171. ——— Surprise and the Psycho-Analyst. New York: E. P. Dutton and Co., 1937.

172. RIVIERE, JOAN: A Contribution to the Analysis of Negative Therapeutic Reaction. Int. J. Psa., XVII, 1936, pp. 304–320.

173. ROBITSEK, ALFRED: Symbolisches Denken in der chemischen Forschung. Imago, I, 1912, pp. 83–90.

174. SACHS, HANNS: Metapsychological Points of View in Technique and Theory. Int. J. Psa., VI, 1925, pp. 5–12.

175. ——— Behavior as an Expression of Mental Process During Analysis. Int. J. Psa., XI, 1930, pp. 231–332.

176. ——— Zur Theorie der psychoanalytischen Technik. Int. Ztschr. Psa., XXIII, 1937, p. 563.

177. SADGER, ISIDOR: *Erfolge und Dauer der psychoanalytischen Neurosenbehandlung.* Int. Ztschr. Psa., XV, 1929, pp. 426–434.

178. SCHMIDEBERG, MELITTA: *Zur Wirkungsweise der psychoanalytischen Therapie.* Int. Ztschr. Psa., XXI, 1935, pp. 46–54.

179. —— *Reassurance as a Means of Analytic Technique.* Int. J. Psa., XVI, 1935, pp. 307–324.

180. —— *The Mode of Operation of Psycho-Analytic Therapy.* Int. J. Psa., XIX, 1938, p. 310 ff.

181. —— *After the Analysis.* The Psa. Quarterly, VII, 1938, pp. 122–142.

182. SCHULTZ-HENCKE, HARALD: *Einführung in die Psychoanalyse.* Jena: Gustav Fischer, 1927.

183. SEARL, M. N.: *Some Queries on Principles of Technique.* Int. J. Psa., XVII, 1936, pp. 471–493.

184. SHARPE, ELLA F.: *The Technique of Psycho-Analysis.* Int. J. Psa., XI, 1930, pp. 251–277; 361–386; XII, 1931, pp. 24–60.

185. SHEEHAN-DARE, HELEN: *On Making Contact with the Child Patient.* Int. J. Psa., XV, 1934, pp. 435–439.

186. SIMMEL, ERNEST: *Psycho-Analytic Treatment in a Clinic.* Int. J. Psa., X, 1929, pp. 70–90.

187. SLUTSKY, ALBERT: *Interpretation of a Resistance: The Analytical Treatment as a Neurotic Defense.* The Psa. Quarterly, I, 1932, pp. 345–448.

188. STEINER, MAXIM: *The Dream Symbolism of the Analytical Situation.* Int. J. Psa., XVIII, 1937, pp. 294–305.

189. STERBA, RICHARD: *Über negative Übertragung.* Int. Ztschr. Psa., XIII, 1927, pp. 160–165.

190. —— *Zur Dynamik der Bewältigung des Übertragungswiderstandes.* Int. Ztschr. Psa., XV, 1929, pp. 456–470. [Eng. trans. The Psa. Quarterly, IX, No. 3, 1940.]

191. —— *The Fate of the Ego in Analytic Therapy.* Int. J. Psa., XV, 1934, pp. 117–126.

192. —— *Das Psychische Trauma und die Handhabung der Übertragung.* Int. Ztschr. Psa., XXII, 1936, pp. 40–58

193. —— *Zur Theorie der Übertragung.* Imago, XXII, 1936, pp. 456–470.

194. STERN, ADOLPH: *On the Counter-Transference in Psychoanalysis.* Psa. Rev., XI, 1924, pp. 166–174.

195. —— *A Psychoanalytic Attempt to Explain Some Spontaneous 'Cures' in the Psycho-Neuroses.* Psa. Rev., XI, 1924, pp. 415–425.

196. —— *What Is a Cure in Psychoanalysis?* Author's Abstract, Psa. Rev., XII, 1925, p. 461.

197. STRACHEY, JAMES: *The Nature of the Therapeutic Action of Psycho-Analysis.* Int. J. Psa., XV, 1934, pp. 127–159.

198. —— *Symposium on the Theory of Therapeutic Results of Psycho-Analysis.* Int. J. Psa., XVIII, 1937, pp. 139–146.

199. TANEYHILL, G. LANE: *Notes on Psychoanalytic Technique.* Psa. Rev., III, 1916, p. 461.

200. WITTELS, FRITZ: *Die Technik der Psychoanalyse.* Munich: Bergmann, 1926.